wake up – it's time
for your sleeping pill

Robert Swiatek

12/05/08

wake up – it's time for your sleeping pill

ROBERT S. SWIATEK

Swiatek Press

Published by Swiatek Press, Inc.
71 Georgian Lane #3
Buffalo, NY 14221

ISBN: 0-9817843-0-5

Printed in the United States

This book is dedicated to my siblings:
Fr. Nicholas (once known as Tom,)
Ken and Pat.

also by Robert S. Swiatek

The Read My Lips Cookbook:
A Culinary Journey of Memorable Meals

Don't Bet On It – a novel

Tick Tock, Don't Stop:
A Manual for Workaholics

for seeing eye dogs only

This Page Intentionally Left Blank
– Just Like the Paychecks of the Workers

I Don't Want to be a Pirate – Writer, maybe

Table of contents

Introduction

Sometime in the early 1980s, I finished writing a book about the English language, *You've Got My Word.* It dealt with words, phrases, expressions and clichés in a humorous light, pointing out the difficulty involved because of all the bizarre rules as well as the easily forgettable exceptions to them. I was somehow convinced that English may be the most challenging of all languages. Someone coming to this country from a foreign land and not familiar with it soon comes to the realization that English is no picnic, even if they have wine and cheese and a basket to put them in. The dictionary and makeup of the language are enough to drive anyone crazy.

Once my manuscript was complete, I felt it was missing something and as a result was never published. In fact, it was never even sent to my agent. Nonetheless, it wasn't forgotten and shortly thereafter, I began a folder of material I found for a book on the dumb things that people say and do. I put the words, "(What) Was I Thinking" on the outside of the folder and from time to time added material that was appropriate.

A few years later – sometime in the 1990s – I started a PC folder with more of the same contents, and in the year 2004, while home recovering from surgery, I decided that I had enough material in those two packets for a book. When I was done, the result was my 2005 book, *for seeing eye dogs only*, which also had a few bits from *You've Got My Word*, since they fit right in. It may have taken a few years, but because of circumstances, I soon realized that despite the book being complete, there was more material available for another similar book.

Much of the material of the 2005 book came from observations, everyday occurrences, newspapers and books I read as well as emails that others sent me. My new folder seemed to be overflowing so much that less than two years later, I had what was very close to a sequel, which I decided to call, *wake up – it's time for your sleeping pill*. At the same time I decided that I would incorporate some of the book that I had written in the 1980s into this work.

The result is a book on the three "L's: language, laughter and lunacy. In early 2007, I submitted the manuscript to the Indie Excellence 2007 Book Awards and in a few months was notified that the book was a finalist, along with my book on the environment, *Take Back the Earth* as well as my second book on work, *This Page Intentionally Left Blank – Just like the Paychecks of the Workers*. Because of this submission, it has taken a few months to bring this book into print. There were a few other difficulties I faced – including what every writer encounters regarding making a book better by never ending revisions – which I won't get into.

Over the years, people continue to say and do dumb things – but they can be very funny. I guess you could call those occurrences comatose calamities. No one is exempt, not even writers. When I think about the first book I published, I can only conclude that *The Read My Lips Cookbook* points out that I too was missing intelligence, as illustrated by some of my adventures in the kitchen. As I pointed out in these books on the subject, this was merely a temporary lapse. In some ways, I could be excused since I was learning and could pass this information on to others as well as give readers a few chuckles at the same time.

As you can tell, I choose book titles on their appropriateness as well as potential appeal to readers. You may not be able to tell a book by the cover, but the title and cover can be the difference between someone buying the book or passing it by. I hadn't thought about the title I chose for my 2008 book in this way before, but somehow the word *sleeping* in the title may well describe some of the people who made it into the book, since many humans seem to be in a state approaching unconsciousness. As of the end of the year 2007, I had already amassed some more instances of elevators that don't go to the top so that it shouldn't be too long before another book of this type gets published. My guess is the year 2009. The title I'm thinking of using is *here's your free gift – send $10 for shipping.*

I really am convinced that a great sense of humor can help you live longer, prevent heart attacks and high blood pressure, and even shorten the recovery period after surgery. It can relieve stress and that's why laughter is such great medicine. It can also make your life a bit better at work as well as at home, with all the challenging situations that arise. Our lives are so hectic that without humor, we seem to have little hope. We need to laugh at ourselves and all that's going on.

I need to thank all those who emailed me the truckload of gems – those who send old stuff or anecdotes that are crude, racist and obscene and just not funny, please fill up someone else's mailbox – as well as those who were participants in all those actions so that I could include them in this work. That last word may not be appropriate as I had a great deal of fun doing it. What more can you ask when you need not direct people to send material when the lunacy and laughs show up by themselves? Granted, all the contributions have to be sorted, incremented, supplemented, pureed, collated and edited into a worthwhile venture. However, that's a task that I didn't mind doing.

My decision to make *wake up – it's time for your sleeping pill* slightly different from my 2005 book had to do with the idea of sequels. First of all, in general, they never are as good as the original and they're too hard to sell. However, many of the ideas and subjects found in *for seeing eye dogs only* remain. This book is longer and I hope – notice I didn't use that word, *hopefully* – you'll get as many laughs as the 2005 work, which even as I write this, people are saying is hysterical.

wake up – it's time for your sleeping pill is intentionally not capitalized in the same way that my first book on baffling behavior wasn't. Besides being written to entertain and enlighten readers, it is also an attempt to illustrate the connection between humor and intelligence. You will still be burdened with plenty of putrid puns as well as other examples of the lunacy of language that should put a smile on your face.

I have included some more quotes, signs, bumper stickers and stories of criminals-in-training as well as young intelligence and the religious stuff, which readers raved about in ***for seeing eye dogs only***. I close the book in the same manner as the aforementioned book with ludicrous questions, reflective of the wit of Steven Wright. Perhaps I should have said, "to be continued." Naturally, there are a few new things, and I have more to say about corporate crooks and the political scene – only because of events during the last few years in our nation's capital. As long as there's material, you might as well use it. I tried to follow the same guidelines to spare embarrassment to the players as well as avoiding litigation, but I walked along the edge of the cliff a bit more than the 2005 book, without falling off.

The craziness of the title should be obvious, but this is not a book about health care. Granted, there is a chapter on "Medical brilliance," which should point out the fact that doctors, nurses and hospital administrators have their mental moments. From your experience, I'm sure you know that. I hope you get a few laughs about the time a laboratory gave me a FIT, which can be found in that same chapter.

I repeat the words on the home page of my web site – with a minor modification – "Humor is the best medicine and it's available even without a referral." Here's to good health and plenty of laughs.

1. Quotes and punitive damages

I begin this book with a few quotes, followed shortly thereafter by some painful puns. The quotes have to do with *beer*. You may not want to start off the day with that nutritious liquid. Instead, wait until it's noon – somewhere. I hope you find these words of wisdom entertaining. If they will help sell more copies, all the better.

"Sometimes when I reflect on all the beer I drink I feel ashamed. Then I look into the glass and think about the workers in the brewery and all of their hopes and dreams. If I didn't drink this beer, they might be out of work and their dreams would be shattered. I think, 'It is better to drink this beer and let their dreams come true than be selfish and worry about my liver.'" – Babe Ruth

"I feel sorry for people who don't drink. When they wake up in the morning, that's as good as they're going to feel all day." – Lyndon B. Johnson

"When I read about the evils of drinking, I gave up reading." – Paul Hornung
I think the gambling came later.

"24 hours in a day, 24 beers in a case. Coincidence? I think not." – L. Mencken
Maybe there's something to say about seven days in a week and a Seven & Seven.

"Beer is proof that God loves us and wants us to be happy." – Benjamin Franklin
He invented quite a few things, but Sam Adams was responsible for the beer, although I heard Ben was a lousy brewmaster.

1

"When we drink, we get drunk. When we get drunk, we fall asleep. When we fall asleep, we commit no sin. When we commit no sin, we go to heaven. So, let's all get drunk and go to heaven!" – George Bernard Shaw

"Beer: helping ugly people have sex since 3000 BC!" – W. C. Fields

"Without question, the greatest invention in the history of mankind is beer. Oh, I grant you that the wheel was also a fine invention, but the wheel does not go nearly as well with pizza." – Dave Barry
However, without a car, going to pick up the beer and the pizza would be more of a challenge.

"Remember, 'I' before 'E', except in Budweiser." – Professor Irwin Corey

"To some it's a six-pack, to me it's a 'support group.' Salvation in a can!" – Leo Durocher

"Well ya see, Norm, it's like this. A herd of buffalo can only move as fast as the slowest buffalo. And when the herd is hunted, it is the slowest and weakest ones at the back that are killed first. This natural selection is good for the herd as a whole, because the general speed and health of the whole group keeps improving by the regular killing of the weakest members. In much the same way, the human brain can only operate as fast as the slowest brain cells. Excessive intake of alcohol, as we know, kills brain cells. But naturally, it attacks the slowest and weakest brain cells first. In this way, regular consumption of beer eliminates the weaker brain cells, making the brain a faster and more efficient machine!" – Cliff Clavin, explaining the 'Buffalo Theory' to his buddy Norm, one night at Cheers.
I always thought that theory had to do with my birthplace.

I'll return to the bar in a later chapter. Some people thrive on puns so I have to include a few here. Even if they're not your favorite type of humor, give then a chance. The chapter will be over before you know it and you may even get a chuckle or two. I'll try to spice them up a bit.

I went to a seafood disco last week...and pulled a mussel.
I was crabby for the next twenty-four hours.

Two antennas met on a roof, fell in love and got married. The ceremony wasn't much, but the reception was excellent.
I wonder if they would have had better luck if they had met on the cable network.

"Doc, I can't stop singing 'The Green, Green Grass of Home.'"
"That sounds like Tom Jones Syndrome."
"Is it common?"
"Well, *It's Not Unusual.*"
Teenagers, you'll have to ask you grandparents about this one.

Two cows are standing next to each other in a field. Daisy says to Dolly, "I was artificially inseminated this morning."
"I don't believe you," says Dolly.
"It's true, no bull!" exclaims Daisy.
Holy Cow!

A man woke up in a hospital after a serious accident. He shouted, "Doctor, doctor, I can't feel my legs!"
The doctor replied, "I know you can't – I've cut off your arms!"
At least he didn't cut off his oxygen supply.

Two fish swim into a concrete wall. The one turns to the other and says, "Dam!"
Apparently, they had a roughy time.

Two Eskimos sitting in a kayak were chilly, so they lit a fire in the craft. Unsurprisingly it sank, proving once again that you can't have your kayak and heat it, too.
They wouldn't have had this problem if they were African Eskimos.

A group of chess enthusiasts checked into a hotel and were standing in the lobby discussing their recent tournament victories. After about an hour, the manager came out of the office and asked them to disperse. "But why," they asked, as they moved off.
"Because, I can't stand chess-nuts boasting in an open foyer."
Why don't you guys hang out in the pawn shop?

She was engaged to a boyfriend with a wooden leg but broke it off.
She should talk – her name was Peg.

He had a photographic memory that was never developed.
He ran out of chemicals.

With her marriage, she got a new name and a dress.
She really wanted a lot amore.

Show me a piano falling down a mineshaft and I'll show you A-flat minor.
That's one miner – whose idol was Nat King Cole – singing the blues, with or without the piano.

4

Every calendar's days are numbered.
Not mine – I use the Roman kind.

A lot of money is tainted – It taint yours and it taint mine.
It belongs to Halliburton, the epitome of being tainted.

An actress saw her first strands of gray hair and thought she'd dye.
When she was done, she split – end of story.

If you have been to my web site and clicked on "cancer cure – essiac link," you know that over the last decade I have had a few surgeries. Consequently, I really hope to never have to go through any more of those operations. You might say that I would like to *bypass surgery.*

2. Young opinions

A few of the sections in *for seeing eye dogs only* dealt with children and their comments. There were also some laughs from church bulletins. Here are some questions related to the Bible with their answers.

What do they call pastors in Germany?
German Shepherds.

Who was the greatest financier in the Bible?
Noah. He was floating his stock while everyone else was in liquidation.
For him, everything wasn't two bad.

Who was the greatest female financier in the Bible?
Pharaoh's daughter. She went down to the bank of the Nile and drew out a little prophet.
She loved music as well as Art – that was his name.

What kind of motor vehicles are in the Bible?
Jehovah drove Adam and Eve out of the Garden in a *Fury*. David's *Triumph* was heard throughout the land. Also, probably a *Honda*, because the apostles were all in one *Accord*.
Because of the perils of drugs, they didn't have the Honda Quaalude, Ford Ecstacy, Ford LSD, Dodge Valium, or the Volkswagen Hasher.

Who was the greatest comedian in the Bible?
Samson. He brought the house down.
This was before he got a gig in the Catskills.

Which Bible character had no parents?
Joshua, son of Nun.
I didn't think the Felicians could get married.

7

What excuse did Adam give to his children as to why he no longer lived in Eden?
Your mother ate us out of house and home.
I wonder if they got back their deposit.

Which servant of God was the most flagrant lawbreaker in the Bible?
Moses, because he broke all Ten Commandments at one time.
Everyone loses his balance from time to time.

Which area of Palestine was especially wealthy?
The area around Jordan. The banks were always overflowing.
This was before the credit unions.

Who is the greatest baby sitter mentioned in the Bible?
David. He rocked Goliath to a very deep sleep.
It would have been even easier for him if the place had a DVD player.

Why didn't they play cards on the Ark?
Because Noah was standing on the deck.
They could have gone to the casino downstairs.

Why is it a sin for a woman to make coffee?
It's in the Bible. It says "Hebrews."

Children are the future of our country, but they also provide us with so much insight. Here are a few of their responses from the classroom. You'll notice I let the child have the last word.

Teacher: John, why are you doing your math multiplication on the floor?
John: You told me to do it without using tables.

Teacher: Maria, go to the map and find North America.
Maria: Here it is.
Teacher: Correct. Now class, who discovered America?
Class: Maria.

Teacher: Why are you late, Frank?
Frank: Because of the sign.
Teacher: What sign?
Frank: The one that says, "School ahead, go slow."

Teacher: Glenn, how do you spell "crocodile?"
Glenn: K-R-O-K-O-D-I-A-L.
Teacher: No, that's wrong
Glenn: Maybe it is wrong, but you asked me how I spell it.

Teacher: Donald, what is the chemical formula for water?
Donald: H I J K L M N O.
Teacher: What are you talking about?
Donald: Yesterday you said it's H to O.

Teacher: Winnie, name one important thing we have today
         that we didn't have ten years ago.
Winnie: Me!

Teacher: Glen, why do you always get so dirty?
Glen: Well, I'm a lot closer to the ground than you are.

Teacher: Millie, give me a sentence starting with "I."
Millie: I is...
Teacher: No, Millie. Always say, "I am."
Millie: All right. I am the ninth letter of the alphabet.

Teacher: George Washington not only chopped down his
         father's cherry tree, but also admitted it. Now, Louie,
         do you know why his father didn't punish him?
Louis: Because George still had the ax in his hand.

9

Teacher: Now, Simon, tell me frankly, do you say prayers before eating?

Simon: No sir, I don't have to, my mom is a good cook.

Teacher: Clyde, your composition on "My Dog" is exactly the same as your brother's. Did you copy his?

Clyde: No, teacher, it's the same dog.

Teacher: Harold, what do you call a person who keeps on talking when people are no longer interested?

Harold: A teacher.

The intelligence of youth can be excused since they are still learning, so here are a few more ideas from them, some with my two cents.

The Sunday School teacher was carefully explaining the story of Elijah the Prophet and the false prophets of Baal. She explained how Elijah built the altar, put wood upon it, cut the steer in pieces, and laid it upon the altar. And then, Elijah commanded the people of God to fill four barrels of water and pour it over the altar. He had them do this four times.

"Now," said the teacher, "can anyone in the class tell me why the Lord would have Elijah pour water over the steer on the altar?"

A little girl in the back of the room started waving her hand, "I know! I know!" she said, "To make the gravy!"

A vegetarian would never have come up with that comment.

The Sunday School teacher was describing how Lot's wife looked back and turned into a pillar of salt, when little Jason interrupted, "My Mummy looked back once, while she was driving," he announced triumphantly, "And she turned into a telephone pole!"

At least she didn't turn into WalMart.

A Sunday School teacher asked, "Johnny, do you think Noah did a lot of fishing when he was on the Ark?"

"No," replied Johnny. "How could he, with just two worms."

No one told him about the flies.

A Sunday School teacher said to her children, "We have been learning how powerful kings and queens were in Bible times. But, there is a higher power. Can anybody tell me what it is?"

One child blurted out, "Aces!"

And you thought Internet poker was a new innovation!

Nine-year-old Joey was asked by his mother what he had learned in Sunday School. "Well, Mom, our teacher told us how God sent Moses behind enemy lines on a rescue mission to lead the Israelites out of Egypt. When he got to the Red Sea, he had his army build a pontoon bridge and all the people walked across safely. Then, he radioed headquarters for reinforcements. They sent bombers to blow up the bridge and all the Israelites were saved."

"Now, Joey, is that really what your teacher taught you?" His mother asked.

"Well, no, mom. But, if I told it the way the teacher did, you'd never believe it!"

A rabbi said to a precocious six-year-old boy, "So your mother says your prayers for you each night? Very commendable. What does she say?"

The little boy replied, "Thank God he's in bed!"

A Sunday School teacher decided to have her young class memorize one of the most quoted passages in the Bible: Psalm 23. She gave the youngsters a month to learn the verse. Little Rick was excited about the task but he just couldn't remember the Psalm. After much practice, he could barely get past the first line.

On the day that the kids were scheduled to recite Psalm 23 in front of the congregation, Ricky was so nervous. When it was his turn, he stepped up to the microphone and said proudly, "The Lord is my Shepherd, and that's all I need to know."

Not if you want to avoid summer school.

The preacher's five year-old daughter noticed that her father always paused and bowed his head, for a moment, before starting his sermon. One day, she asked him why.

"Well, Honey," he began, proud that his daughter was so observant of his messages, "I'm asking the Lord to help me preach a good sermon."

"How come He doesn't do it?" she asked.

I hope she can go a few days without dessert.

Our son had only heard his grandfather pray at Thanksgiving, Easter, and other special occasions when he, typically, said a long prayer over the food.

One night, after a fun camp-out and fishing trip, grandfather – to our son's surprise – asked for a very brief blessing on the food. With a gleam in his eye, our son grinned at his grandfather and said, "You don't pray so long when you're hungry, do you Grandpa?"

Rubba dub dub, thanks for the grub, dear God!

During the minister's prayer one Sunday, there was a loud whistle from one of the back pews.

Gary's mother was horrified. She pinched him into silence and, after church, asked, "Gary, whatever made you do such a thing?"

Gary answered, soberly, "I asked God to teach me to whistle – and He just then did!"

12

A pastor asked a little boy if he said his prayers every night.

"Yes sir," the boy replied.

"And, do you always say them in the morning, too?" the pastor asked.

"No sir," the boy replied. "I ain't scared in the daytime."

He never went quail hunting with Cheney.

My wife invited some people to dinner. At the table, she turned to our six-year-old daughter and said, "Would you like to say the blessing?"

"I wouldn't know what to say," she replied.

"Just say what you hear Mommy say," my wife said.

Our daughter bowed her head and said, "Dear Lord, why on earth did I invite all these people to dinner?"

At least she won't have to cook for them again.

One particular four-year-old prayed, "And forgive us our 'trash baskets' as we forgive those who put trash in our baskets."

These people are going to way too many yard sales.

When my daughter, Kelli, was three, she and my son, Cody, would say their nightly prayers, together. As most children do, we have to bless every customer, every friend, and every animal, current and past.

For several weeks, after we had finished the nightly prayer, Kelli would say, "And all girls."

As this soon became part of her nightly routine to include those three words at the end, my curiosity got the best of me and I asked her, "Kelli, why do you always add the part about all girls?"

Her response, "Because we always finish our prayers by saying 'All men!'"

13

Little Johnny and his family were having Sunday dinner at his grandmother's house. Everyone was seated around the table as the food was being served. When little Johnny received his plate, he started eating right away.

"Johnny, wait until we say our prayer."

"I don't have to," The boy replied.

"Of course, you do," his mother insisted. "We say a prayer, before eating, at our house."

"That's our house," Johnny explained. "But this is Grandma's house and she knows how to cook."

Little did he know that his mother had a few new recipes planned for him at home.

I received the following email from my sister, Pat, before Christmas in 2006. These may not all be legitimate, but they are funny. Because of some of the crude comments on Santa's part – he must have had a tough year – I have taken the liberty of substituting a few words here and there, but I left in the misspellings.

Dear Santa,

I wud like a kool toy space ranjur fer Xmas. Iv ben a gud boy all yeer.

Yer Frend,

BiLLy

Dear Billy,

Nice spelling. You're on your way to a career in lawn care. How about I send you a frigging book so you can learn to read and write? I'm giving your older brother the space ranger. At least HE can spell!

Santa

I didn't know Santa was a sailor.

Dear Santa,

I have been a good girl all year, and the only thing I ask for is peace and joy in the world for everybody!

Love,
Sarah

Dear Sarah,

Your parents smoked pot when they had you, didn't they?

Santa

I always wondered what was in the pipe that he was smoking.

Dear Santa,

I don't know if you can do this, but for Christmas, I'd like for my Mommy and Daddy to get back together. Please see what you can do.

Love,
Teddy

Dear Teddy,

Look, your dad's been playing a symphony with the babysitter for months now, and he's tone deaf. Do you think he's gonna give that up to come back to your frigid, fat mom, who rides his buddha constantly? It's time to give up that dream. Let me get you some nice Legos instead. Maybe you can build yourself a family with those.

Santa

Dear Santa,

I left milk and cookies for you under the tree, and I left carrots for your reindeer outside the back door.

Love,
Susan

15

Dear Susan,

Milk for me means I'll have to wear brown pants and that wouldn't match my coat. Carrots make the deer flatulate in my face when riding in the sleigh – if you're not sure what that word means, look it up. Didn't you see the marble rye episode on Seinfeld? You want to do me a favor? Two words, Jim Beam.

Santa

You probably shouldn't leave him Bailey's Irish Cream, either.

Dear Santa,

What do you do the other 364 days of the year? Are you busy making toys?

Your friend,
Thomas

Dear Thomas,

All the toys are made by little kids like you in China. Every year I give them a slice of bread as a Christmas bonus. I have a condo in Vegas, where I spend most of my time making low-budget porno films. I unwind by drinking myself silly and squeezing the behinds of cocktail waitresses while losing money at the craps table.

P.S. Tell your mom she got the part.

Long Dong Claus

I wonder if he does any bell ringing for the Salvation Army.

Dear Santa,

Do you see us when we're sleeping, do you really know when we're awake, like in the song?

Love,
Jessica

16

Dear Jessica,

>Are you really that gullible? Do you think I work for the CIA? I tried to get a job there but they wouldn't hire me because of the red suit.
>Santa

Dear Santa,

>I really, really want a puppy this year. Please, please please, PLEASE, PLEASE could I have one?
>Timmy

Timmy,

>How about one of my reindeer? He's been slacking off so I'll just leave him at your house and I won't have to fire him.
>Santa

Dearest Santa,

>We don't have a chimney in our house, how do you get into our home?
>Love,
>Marky

Mark,

>First, stop calling yourself "Marky", that's why you're getting your rear kicked at school. Second, I'd probably get my butt stuck, so I wouldn't be coming down your chimney if you had one. I'll get in with my credit card.
>Sweet Dreams,
>Santa

Santa could have told him to contact Home Depot for a chimney and buy some grease.

I close the chapter with a reading from the Bible – well, almost.

In The Beginning

In the beginning God covered the earth with broccoli and cauliflower and spinach, green and yellow and red vegetables of all kinds, so man and woman would live long and healthy lives. Then using God's bountiful gifts, Satan created Ben and Jerry's and Krispy Kreme.

And Satan said, "You want chocolate with that?"

And Man said, "Yes!"

And Woman said, "I'll have another with sprinkles." And they gained ten pounds.

And God created the healthful yogurt that Woman might keep the figure that Man found so fair. And Satan brought forth white flour from the wheat, and sugar from the cane, and combined them. And Woman went from size two to size six.

So God said, "Try my fresh green salad." And Satan presented Thousand-Island dressing and garlic toast on the side. And Man and Woman unfastened their belts following the repast.

God then said, "I have sent you heart healthy vegetables and olive oil in which to cook them." And Satan brought forth deep fried shrimp and catfish and chicken-fried steak so big it needed its own platter. And Man gained more weight and his cholesterol went through the roof.

God then brought forth running shoes so that his children might lose those extra pounds. And Satan came forth with a cable TV with remote control so Man would not have to toil changing the channels. And Man and Woman laughed and cried before the flickering light and piled on the pounds.

Then God brought forth the potato, naturally low in fat and brimming with potassium and good nutrition. Then

Satan peeled off the healthful skin and sliced the starchy center into chips and deep-fried them and added copious quantities of salt. And Man put on more pounds.

God then gave lean beef so that Man might consume fewer calories and still satisfy his appetite. And Satan created McDonald's and the 99-cent double cheeseburger.

Then Lucifer said, "You want fries with that?"

And Man replied, "Yes! And super size 'em!"

And Satan said, "It is good." And Man went into cardiac arrest.

God sighed and created quadruple bypass surgery.

And Satan created HMOs.

3. No need to worry about getting brainwashed

As far as I can tell, "dumbness" isn't a word, just yet. Give it time. It's what this book and my first book on intelligence follies are all about. An assumption is made that this quality exists and gives credence to the "For Dummies" series. There may not be a **Breathing For Dummies** or **Walking For Dummies** book, but I remember hearing about some health or exercise magazine that described about twenty ways of walking. I didn't think there were that many choices – you put one foot forward, then the other and repeat the process. It's not that difficult.

Stupidity is everywhere, even if only of a temporary kind. But even that type can drive people crazy and give us all a few laughs. Here are just a few cases of this affliction.

You probably heard about the hybrid SUV. What did they cross it with, a Hummer? With this wonderful idea, the next thing we might see is an environmentally friendly Humvee.
Our model gets 10 gallons to the mile.

One of the places where I see too much lunacy is out on the highways and byways. A later chapter gets into some of the crazy signs you see throughout the day, but there is an even more troublesome feature – drivers. I always thought a person needed some intelligence to get a driver's license but maybe it came as a bonus with the book club. People drive like maniacs to get to work and then sit around all morning drinking coffee. On all too many occasions I have had amateurs pass me and then a short time later I would see them waiting at the light for the signal to turn from red to green as I approached, and then I'd see them again further down the road at another light.

I'm sure this has happened to you. You'll be out on the interstate when some duphus – from the Latin, or is it doofus? – flies past at fifteen miles over the speed limit, and there's ice or snow on the highway. Just because there is a speed limit doesn't mean you have to actually drive it, especially if conditions aren't that great. A mile later you see the same vehicle in the center median, except it's lying upside down. You may want to wave to him as you pass.

With each passing day, it gets more difficult to find food to eat that isn't tainted. Fish is supposedly better for you than beef or pork, but with all the mercury and poisons in the oceans, lakes and streams, I'm not so sure. There is one species of fish that you may have heard of – the puffer fish. It has a few other names as well. If you have no knowledge of it, let me just mention that unless it is properly prepared, you will die from it. Here I emphasize that the final result under the wrong circumstances will not be sickness, but death.

If you go to a restaurant and ask about the puffer entrée, the waiter might say, "So far, none of our patrons have died at the hands of our chef." To me that is very reassuring. Customers still order the dish and put their fate in the hands of the guy in the kitchen. I have one question: What else is on the menu?

The war in Iraq was initiated to defeat terrorism. It ended in 2003, supposedly – remember the sign, *Mission Accomplished*? If that is the case, why is President George W. Bush asking for more money for the effort? Am I missing something here? Come on, Congress, don't approve the funds and use them here at home
Maybe the sign mentioned is a reference to Halliburton.

With regard to the war, the missing intelligence gets much worse. But let us hear from someone else in the matter.

22

Paul Freundlich put it at the start of that illogical, unjust and unnecessary war begun in 2003.

"All right, let me see if I understand the logic of this correctly. We are going to ignore the United Nations in order to make clear to Saddam Hussein that the United Nations cannot be ignored. We're going to wage war to preserve the U.N.'s ability to avert war. The paramount principle is that the U.N.'s word must be taken seriously, and if we have to subvert its word to guarantee that it is, then, by gum, we will. Peace is too important not to take up arms to defend. Am I getting this right?"

From a financial point of view, war is lunacy. It costs trillions of dollars and that may be a gross underestimate. How about sitting down and negotiating with the enemy – whoever that happens to be. You can probably wind up with a payment of a few billion bucks and save the lives of hundreds of thousands of people at the same time. It would also work wonders in the area of human relations. The environment would be much better off and the money saved could be put to great use. There is some bad news: the undertakers, banks and weapons manufacturers won't be able to line their pockets as well.

More lunacy comes about when the call for war is accompanied by tax cuts. To make matters even worse – this is not funny at all – these go to the rich. These wealthy citizens not only don't have any use for this gesture, but they don't want it. Well, that's not true of all of them – some greedy people can never have enough.

It certainly isn't at all funny but how did so many in Congress give a yes vote way back when? Anyone with the least snippet of brains would have questioned the wars in both Afghanistan and Iraq. After all, didn't the country not that long ago suffer the agony of defeat in Vietnam? Apparently those in Washington forgot all about that debacle. Those who supported these fiascos were guilty of

23

shutting down their intelligence rather than serving their country. A rutabaga could figure out that you can't fight terrorism by conventional means.

There's more missing intelligence when ordinary people as well as those in politics do some fancy talking – this implies that politicians aren't normal. Believe it or not – despite the 11% approval rating of the Congress as I write this – there are some decent people in Washington, DC. Do people who pass off lies to others believe that listeners aren't that intelligent? Haven't they got the slightest clue that their untruths will be found out, soon enough? This effort may not be funny, but it's just plain dumb.

I personally feel that the height of stupidity can be seen daily on television. Marketing has to embody all I pointed out in the paragraph above. In my view, *false advertising* has become a pleonasm. If you don't know what that word means, you better look it up. It will come up again later in the book.

Unfortunately, any commercial you view will probably show lack of creativity, crassness and the only reason it is on the air is to sell a product, regardless of its efficacy. Some of the better claims have to do with drugs. I doubt that there are any without side effects, even my fictitious sleeping pill.

Sleepeze will give you more restless sleep. Side effects include drowsiness, nausea, headache, occasional neuralgia, coma and in some very rare instances, death. You could also feel the desire to sit in a room with insurance salesmen. Those using it should not be in close contact with farm animals. Use only with a doctor's approval.

Bungee jumping has got to be high on the list of adventures that I can do without, rating right up there with climbing walls of ice and walking on a rope stretched over

Niagara Falls. Perhaps the jumping can be made a bit safer by doing it over water. Of course, that won't matter if there are numerous rocks below the surface or if the diver can't swim. There is one other problem that has happened. The cord was strong enough so it didn't break but it was too long. *Water may have helped in this situation.*

Acronyms are a real **PITA**. If you can't figure that one out, the first three words are, *Pain In The.* I have created a few that I hope give you a laugh or two.

CONGRESS – Completely Oblivious Not Grasping Reality Erasing Social Security

IBM – I've Been Moved or Itsy Bitsy Minds or I've Been Manipulated

I think the last one applies. Recently I tried to get some web design software, put out by IBM. To begin with, I talked to the company that sent me the software and they gave me a phone number for IBM with an option number to select. I dialed the number and before too long I was transferred four times to someone who could help me. In the last case, the phone rang and rang and eventually I heard, "The party you are trying to reach is not available. Try again later."

It gets even worse. Eventually I tried again and got through to someone and asked for companies in the area from which I could buy the software I wanted. I was given five establishments with phone numbers. When I called the first, I was told they didn't sell that stuff. It turns out they were a consulting company. It didn't take me too long to realize that all the other four places were the same type of company and couldn't help me.

WOOFS – Well-Off Older Folks

IRS – Irritate Retired Seniors
Alternatively and more personally, Irritate Robert Swiatek

WIMP – Waffling Ignorant Machiavellian Politician

ETC – el toro crappo
This really seems appropriate. From now on, every time you see this acronym, you should smile. On a few occasions you will break out laughing.

TGIF - This Goes In Front
Very useful for some people when they put on fresh underwear.

RALPH – Really Annoying Loud Pathetic Human
Kramden, not Kramer

SITCOM – Single Income, Two Children, Oppressive Mortgage. What yuppies turn into when they have children and one of them stops working to stay home with the kids

WOLFS – Well-Off Lecherous Folks

FBI – Finding Bush's Irritants

TSOP – This Stuff Only Proliferates
The second word can be replaced with a more common word that you all know.

In a period of a week or so during the fall of 2006, I have been getting a few phone calls that indicate a lack of intelligence, even if only temporary. I can only assume that these are from telemarketers even if they are asking for a contribution. After all, the caller is on the phone and doing marketing. I think that this category of person deserves

26

recognition. The said callers reach my answering machine and then hear my very short, recorded response to leave a message. What I have heard more times than learned people need to hear are the words, "Hello . . .hello," or on a few other occasions, "Mr. Swee-ah-teck – that's how it sounded – (short delay) Mr. Swee-ah-teck." Apparently, besides training the callers on the use of the telephone, a lesson is also needed on the role of answering machines, which they may not have heard of.

Be sure and cancel your credit cards before you die. If you figure out how to do that, let me know. This is so priceless, and so easy to see happening, customer service being what it is today. A lady died, and a bank – reputedly, Citibank – billed her for February and March for their annual service charges on her credit card, and added late fees and interest on the monthly charge. The balance had been zero, but now it was somewhere around sixty dollars. A customer placed a call to the bank and here's the exchange:

Customer: "I am calling to tell you she died in January."
Bank: "The account was never closed and the late fees and charges still apply."
Customer: "Maybe, you should turn it over to collections."
Bank: "Since it is two months past due, it already has been."
Customer: "So, what will they do when they find out she is dead?"
Bank: "Either report her account to frauds division or report her to the credit bureau, maybe both."
Customer: "Do you think God will be mad at her?"
Bank: "Excuse me?"
Customer: "Did you just get what I was telling you the part about her being dead?"
Bank: "Sir, you'll have to speak to my supervisor."
Customer: "I'm calling to tell you, she died in January."

Supervisor: "The account was never closed, so the late fees and charges still apply." (This must be a phrase taught by the bank.)

Customer: "Do you mean you want to collect from her estate?"

Supervisor: (Stammering) "Are you her lawyer?"

Customer: "No, I'm her great nephew."

Supervisor: "Could you fax us a certificate of death?"

Customer: "Sure."

The fax number is given and here is the conversation after they get the fax.

Supervisor: "Our system just isn't set up for death. I don't know what more I can do to help."

Customer: "Well, if you figure it out, great. If not, you could just keep billing her. I really don't think she will care."

Supervisor: "Well, the late fees and charges do still apply."

Customer: "Would you like her new billing address?"

Supervisor: "Yes, that will help."

Customer: "Odessa Memorial Cemetery, Highway 129, Plot number 69."

Supervisor: "Sir, that's a cemetery."

Customer: "What do you do with dead people on your planet?

Hire them at the bank.

The following are supposedly genuine. From my experience, I have little doubt that they are.

Dispatcher: 911 – what is your emergency?

Caller: I heard what sounded like gunshots coming from the brown house on the corner.

Dispatcher: Do you have an address?

Caller: No, I have on a blouse and slacks, why?

They shot the wrong person.

28

Dispatcher: 911 – what is the nature of your emergency?

Caller: I'm trying to reach nine eleven but my phone doesn't have an eleven on it.

Dispatcher: This is nine eleven.

Caller: I thought you just said it was nine one one.

Dispatcher: Yes, ma'am, nine one one and nine eleven are the same thing.

Caller: Honey, I may be old, but I'm not stupid.

I would have told her to head over to Circuit City for a phone with an eleven on it.

Dispatcher: 911 – what is your emergency?

Caller: Someone broke into my house and took a bite out of my ham and cheese sandwich.

Dispatcher: Excuse me?

Caller: I made a ham and cheese sandwich and left it on the kitchen table and when I came back from the bathroom, someone had taken a bite out of it.

Dispatcher: Was anything else taken?

Caller: No, but this has happened to me before and I'm sick and tired of it!

Dispatcher: 911.

Caller: Yeah, I'm having trouble breathing. I'm all out of breath. Darn – I think I'm going to pass out.

Dispatcher: Sir, where are you calling from?

Caller: I'm at a pay phone. North and Foster.

Dispatcher: Sir, an ambulance is on the way. Are you an asthmatic?

Caller: No.

Dispatcher: What were you doing before you started having trouble breathing?

Caller: Running from the Police.

4. Worthless facts

You may have earned a degree and have some knowledge. Thus you may think you know everything. Just one second, *soy brain*. Here are a few things you probably didn't know. They really aren't all that funny so I added a few thoughts.

A dime has 118 ridges around the edge.
Who had the time to count them?

A cat has 32 muscles in each ear.
But can they bench press?

A crocodile cannot stick out its tongue.
It doesn't need to, so beware.

A dragonfly has a life span of 24 hours.
Unfortunately, the same can't be said for suicide bombers, but they come close.

A goldfish has a memory span of three seconds.
How does this compare to that of some businessmen?

A "jiffy" is an actual unit of time for 1/100th of a second.
I always thought it was peanut butter.

The glue on Israeli postage stamps is certified kosher.
Susan and George should have bought wedding invitations with this glue on the envelopes.

A shark is the only fish that can blink with both eyes.
I'm not sure if this was true for George Schultz, but I know he could talk without moving his lips.

A snail can sleep for three years.
Reagan broke that record in office.

An ostrich's eye is bigger than its brain.
That applies to the eyes of telemarketers.

Al Capone's business card said he was a used furniture dealer.
I wonder if he might have gotten more business if it said "bank thief."

All fifty states are listed across the top of the Lincoln Memorial on the back of the five-dollar bill.
I think you can also find them in Bubba's tattoo.

An almond is a member of the peach family.
Bankers are members of the dodo family. Sorry, I didn't mean to offend that bird.

Babies are born without kneecaps. They don't appear until the child reaches two to six years of age.
That's why they can't use the kneeler in church for a few years.

Butterflies taste with their feet.
So do Italians making wine.

Cats have over one hundred vocal sounds. Dogs only have about ten.
I've known people with pets that had more sounds, but these people didn't like animals. For SPCA people and animal lovers, it's a joke.

The "spot" on 7UP comes from its inventor, who had red eyes. He was albino.
Maybe that's why the drink isn't the color of Coke or Pepsi.

Forty percent of McDonald's profits come from the sales of Happy Meals.
*If you've read **Fast Food Nation** or seen the movie, **Super Size Me**, you should realize that too many of these will result in very little happiness, health wise.*

Donald Duck comics were banned from Finland because he doesn't wear pants.
When Don went to the mall, they were sold out except for a few pair that he didn't like.

Money isn't made out of paper; it's made out of cotton.
That was especially true in the South before the Civil War.

"Dreamt" is the only English word that ends in the letters "mt."
Those two letters also describe many corporate executives' brains.

It's impossible to sneeze with your eyes open.
I hope that wasn't the result of a government study.

February 1865 is the only month in recorded history not to have a full moon.
Guys in trench coats changed that, but I'm not sure if they were full.

In the last 4,000 years, no new animals have been domesticated.
This doesn't include Oakland Raider fans.

If the population of China walked past you in a single file, the line would never end because of the rate of reproduction.
Who would be left to cook dinner in Peking?

If you are an average American, in your whole life, you will spend an average of six months waiting at red lights.
No wonder it takes me so long to get home from work.

A raisin dropped in a glass of fresh champagne will bounce up and down continuously from the bottom of the glass to the top.
After a half hour it becomes a grape.

Most lipstick contains fish scales.
I figured that was true for talipia and wide-mouth bass.

Leonardo da Vinci invented scissors. Also, it took him ten years to paint Mona Lisa's lips.
It would have taken less time if they weren't covered with those fish scales.

Maine is the only state whose name is just one syllable.
What about 'Raq?

No word in the English language rhymes with month, orange, silver, or purple.
Two words rhyme with orange – "door hinge." Isn't "tillver" a farm instrument used for turning over the soil? Wasn't Zorro's horse named, "Zilver?" You heard him say, "Hi Ho, Zilver." What about "burpull?" That's a tug of war between two beer-chugging fraternities.

Rubber bands last longer when refrigerated.
So do Senators.

Ketchup was sold in the 1830's as medicine.
Not that many years ago it was declared a vegetable – and that's no joke.

On a Canadian two dollar bill, the flag flying over the Parliament building is an American flag.
By now, it has probably been removed.

Our eyes are always the same size from birth, but our nose and ears never stop growing.
Obesity in this country might indicate these aren't the only things.

Peanuts are one of the ingredients of dynamite.
Why were there no explosions on Jimmy Carter's farm?

"Stewardesses" is the longest word typed with only your left hand and "lollipop" with your right.
"A" is the shortest word typed with only the left hand and "I" with your right, but who cares?

The average person's left hand does 56% of the typing.
That's not true in my case – maybe I'm not average.

The cruise liner, QE2, moves only six inches for each gallon of diesel fuel that it burns.
That's more than 10,000 gallons to the mile. Put a sail on it.

There are only four words in the English language that end in "dous": tremendous, horrendous, stupendous, and hazardous.
They forgot kudous.

The sentence: "The quick brown fox jumps over the lazy dog" uses every letter of the alphabet.
Knowing that will come in handy in graduate school.

The microwave was invented after a researcher walked by a radar tube and a chocolate bar melted in his pocket.
Fortunately, he didn't have M&Ms.

The winter of 1932 was so cold that Niagara Falls froze completely solid.
That was good for skating at the winter carnival that year.

The words *racecar*, *kayak* and *level* are the same whether they are read left to right or right to left.
But not upside down.

There are 293 ways to make change for a dollar.
There are other combinations, but you'll probably get arrested.

There are more chickens than people in the world.
There also are more "chicken hawks" than people in government.

There are two words in the English language that have all five vowels in order: "abstemious" and "facetious."
The Polish spelling of farm comes close – EIEIO. If you don't get it, think Old MacDonald.

There's no Betty Rubble in the Flintstones Chewable Vitamins.
Someone needs to find a hobby or for God's sake, put Betty in the jar.

The Declaration of Independence was written on hemp paper.
Isn't that justification for legalizing marijuana? It's in the Declaration of Independence.

Tigers have striped skin, not just striped fur.
I never got close enough to look, nor do I intend to.

Typewriter is the longest word that can be made using the letters only on one row of the keyboard.
This statement won't be true in a few years, with the way intelligence is progressing.

Winston Churchill was born in a ladies' room during a dance.
Wasn't there enough room on the ballroom floor?

Women blink nearly twice as much as men.
They also seem to spend money twice as fast.

On average, twelve newborns will be given to the wrong parents, daily.
No wonder the health care industry has problems.

Your stomach has to produce a new layer of mucus every two weeks; otherwise it will digest itself.
If only we could prevent mucus production in the stomachs of people at the IRS.

Leonardo da Vinci could write with one hand and draw with the other at the same time and thus multi-tasking was invented.
He had trouble shooting layups from the left side.

Upper and lower case letters are named 'upper' and 'lower' because in the time when all original print had to be set in individual letters, the upper case letters were stored in the case on top of the case that stored the smaller, lower case letters.
*It was different in the military as the result was the **upper GI** and **lower GI** series.*

37

By raising your legs slowly and lying on your back, you can't sink in quicksand.
That probably won't work if you're stuck in a vat of chocolate.

Chocolate affects a dog's heart and nervous system; a few ounces will kill a small-sized dog.
It didn't seem to bother Farfel. You'll probably have to ask your parents to explain who Farfel is.

Orca whales kill sharks by torpedoing up into the shark's stomach from underneath, causing the shark to explode.
Who said sharks had an easy life?

Because metal was scarce, the Oscars given out during World War II were made of wood.
*That would have been appropriate if **Child's Play** or **A Nightmare on Elm Street** ever won an award.*

The first product Motorola started to develop was a record player for automobiles. At that time, the most known player on the market was the Victrola, so they called themselves Motorola.
Had this been implemented, DJs would have been mixing music a lot sooner.

Chewing gum while peeling onions will keep you from crying.
Putting the gum into the dish makes the food chewier.

The Guinness Book of Records holds the record for being the book most often stolen from Public Libraries.
Despite this, not enough copies have been stolen.

I'm not sure if these will work, but here are a few household suggestions:

Put a sealed envelope in the freezer for a few hours and then slide a knife under the flap. The envelope can then be resealed.
Ashcroft probably knew about this.

You can use empty toilet paper rolls to store appliance cords as it keeps them neat and you can write on the roll which appliance it belongs to.
Put your ears in them when you go for your draft physical and you probably won't have to serve.

For icy door steps in freezing temperatures, get warm water and put Dawn dishwashing liquid in it. Pour it all over the steps. They won't refreeze.
You can't use this idea at dusk.

To remove old wax from a glass candle holder, put it in the freezer for a few hours. Then take the candle holder out and turn it upside down. The wax will fall out.
This probably won't work in the case of ear wax.

To remove crayon marks from walls, use a damp rag, dipped in baking soda and the marks will comes off with little effort.
It might be easier if you just hide the crayons from your husband.

For a permanent marker on appliances or counter tops – like store receipt blue – use rubbing alcohol on a paper towel.
I'm not sure if using gin will work, but you can drink it and forget about the cleaning.

Someone sent in this suggestion. Whenever I purchase a box of S.O.S Pads, I immediately take a pair of scissors and cut each pad into halves. After years of having to throw away rusted and unused and smelly pads, I finally decided that this would be much more economical. Now a box of these pads lasts me indefinitely. In fact, I have noticed that the scissors get "sharpened" this way.
Do people actually put their noses to those things?

If you are stuck with blood stains on clothes, don't worry. Just pour a little hydrogen peroxide on a cloth and proceed to wipe off every drop of blood. Works every time. I have no advice about where to put the body.
I liked Jerry Seinfeld's solution. If this is your problem, you or your beloved are in the wrong profession.

Use vertical strokes when washing windows outside and horizontal for inside windows. This way you can tell which side has the streaks. Straight vinegar will get outside windows really clean. Don't wash windows on a sunny day. They will dry too quickly and will probably streak.
Can you actually buy gay vinegar? I'm not sure my reply will get past the censor.

Spray a bit of perfume on the light bulb in any room to create a lovely light scent in each room when the light is turned on.
What have you been cooking, sauerkraut, Limburger cheese, chili and burritos?

Candles will last a lot longer if placed in the freezer for at least three hours prior to burning.
This also works with a spouse, from what I'm told, but don't ignite.

Place fabric softener sheets in dresser drawers and your clothes will smell freshly washed for weeks to come. You can also do this with towels and linen.

Some time ago, someone wrote a letter to Dear Abby and said they just loved the smell of a man after he had returned from a hard day's work. I prefer the softener sheets.

To clean artificial flowers, pour some salt into a paper bag and add the flowers. Shake vigorously as the salt will absorb all the dust and dirt and leave your artificial flowers looking like new. Works like a charm.

Won't the flowers get high blood pressure?

To easily remove burnt-on food from your skillet, simply add a drop or two of dish soap and enough water to cover the bottom of pan, and bring it to a boil on the stove top.

*You may also want to pick up a copy of **The Read My Lips Cookbook** or take cooking lessons.*

Spray your Tupperware with nonstick cooking spray before pouring in tomato-based sauces and there won't be any stains.

Would this cooking spray have helped Clinton?

Wrap celery in aluminum foil when putting in the refrigerator and it will keep for weeks.

If you have wilted carrots, tie them in knots, put them in cold water and they should be rigid again. Serve with a vegetable dip and your guests will be overwhelmed.

When boiling corn on the cob, add a pinch of sugar to help bring out the corn's natural sweetness.

This didn't work when I tried this on my date. I haven't heard from her in a while.

To cure a headache, take a lime, cut it in half, and rub it on your forehead. The throbbing will go away.
You also won't get scurvy, but remove it before going out in public.

Don't throw out any leftover wine, but instead freeze into ice cubes for future use in casseroles and sauces.
Warning: the parrot in the freezer might get intoxicated.

To get rid of itch from mosquito bites, try applying soap on the area and you will experience instant relief.
You may want to avoid vacations to the tropics.

If ants seem to be everywhere in your home, try this advice since those critters are said to never cross a chalk line. Just get your chalk out and draw a line on the floor or wherever ants tend to march. See for yourself.
You can also play hopscotch in the kitchen.

Use air-freshener to clean mirrors. It does a good job and better still, leaves a lovely smell to the shine.
Too many people are sniffing mirrors.

When you get a splinter, reach for the scotch tape before resorting to tweezers or a needle. Simply put the scotch tape over the splinter, and then pull it off. Scotch tape removes most splinters painlessly and easily.
If you want the splinter removed and aren't concerned about pain, call Uncle Ernie. I'm not sure what to do if you're Irish.

Now look what you can do with Alka Seltzer. Clean a toilet. Drop in two tablets, wait twenty minutes, brush and flush. The citric acid and effervescent action clean vitreous China. You can also clean a vase. To remove a stain from the bottom of a glass vase or cruet, fill with water and

drop in two Alka Seltzer tablets. Clean a thermos bottle by filling the bottle with water, drop in four tablets, and let soak for an hour or more, as necessary. To clean jewelry, drop two tablets into a glass of water and immerse the jewelry for two minutes.
To clean Polish jewelry, use Alski Selski.

Drop three Alka Seltzer tablets down the drain followed by a cup of white vinegar. Wait a few minutes, then run the hot water and the drain will be unclogged.
The drain won't have an upset stomach, either.

Now you know everything, but I'm sure you don't care.

5. Nevermind!

"Truthiness" is the quality of stating concepts one wishes or believes to be true, rather than the facts. The American Dialect Society, a panel of linguists, used the word to best reflect the year 2005. This book has many instances of just that idea.

The words and expressions in this chapter do not exactly fill that quality, but they come close. Thus, I have invented a new word: Websterness. The term that I heard years ago that also seemed to fit was "daffynitions." These are creations by people who take a certain situation and come up with a new word or phrase for it. Many of these are quite clever. I hope you get a few laughs.

repossessed – what will happen if you don't pay your exorcist

Dijon vu – the same mustard as before

Barry Barry – not a new juice drink but rather political déjà vu in Washington, DC

Pope John Paul George Ringo I – the first Beatle pope

acupuncture – a sticky business

svenjolly – don't be fooled by his smiles and good nature

shotgun wedding – a case of wife or death

hangover – the wrath of grapes

dancing cheek-to-cheek – a form of floor play

a will – a dead giveaway

45

Shear Lunacy – a new salon that just opened but you may want to avoid for obvious reasons

correspondunce – aptly describes most of the email I get

scum remover – I tried it once on a town board member, but he's still around

spittune – the receptacle for what comes out of the mouth of a phlegmboyant singer

poultry in motion – a chicken crossing the road
Is it true that some Congressman would make a proposal for walkways for these fowl except that it doesn't qualify as "pork?"

Zorrostan – a sleeping aid for people with capes, black masks and swords

Fuddistan – new on the market and currently producers are trying to determine what it's for, but it can cause dwowsiness

Reekcola – foul smelling soft drink that nonetheless relieves sore throats

Vonage – I see this word on the Internet but am not sure what it is; it probably has something to do with *Wheel of Fortune*

blamestorming – sitting around in a group, discussing why a deadline was missed or a project failed, and who was responsible
Does this sound familiar?

a plateau – a high form of flattery

46

cinonym – word for a spice that is similar to another

Ray leaves – what Rachael uses to spice up soups and stews

ABBA Ghraib – Swedish nightclub where the patrons
    complain that listening to the music is torture
*On some of the selections, the group performed an
extraordinary rendition.*

Irreligious Wrong – more fitting name given to a group that
    once called itself the Religious Right

etiquit – the attitude of many who are disgusted with human
    behavior and have given up

the Karl Rover – new behemoth SUV that steamrolls those
    on their way to the White House or Congress

seagull manager – a manager, who flies in, makes a lot of
    noise, leave a deposit, then leaves
*Maybe, I've been away from the business world too long –
I'm not familiar with this term. I'm really glad I left.*

assmoses – the process by which some people seem to
    absorb success and advancement by kissing up to the
    boss rather than working hard
*This term is not to be confused with **Askmoses** – relying on
someone for advice in order to profit.*

salmon day – the experience of spending an entire day
    swimming upstream only to get screwed and die in
    the end
*This is supposedly a new business phrase. It's no wonder
corporate America is so messed up.*

Vioxx con Dios – this is definitely not the way to go

geniealogy – family tree for individuals living in bottles who grant you wishes

correspondunce – relating to many in the press

swipeout – an ATM or credit card that has been rendered useless because the magnetic strip is worn away from extensive use

infoemation – knowledge the FBI gets on the enemy

apple pan Doody – Clarabelle's favorite dessert

irritainment - entertainment and media spectacles that are annoying but you find yourself unable to stop watching them
Isn't that what all of television has become?

Klaus Barbie doll – newest in a line of dolls that is aimed at the meat market demographic

winoplasty – surgery to improve a facial feature that was affected by drinking too much alcohol

Kikkomanistan – small Russian republic whose sole product is soy sauce

Know Nothing Party – new name given to the merging of the Democratic and Republican Parties

B flatulence – singing this way in church will result in the vocalist winding up in the pew
My Godmother, who passed away a few years ago, was cool. Whenever it appeared that someone had cut the cheese – that was our term for it – she would ask, "Who fluffed?" Maybe that's why I never was fond of that marshmallow stuff.

48

Generica – features of the American landscape, such as fast food joints, strip malls, and subdivisions that are exactly the same no matter where one is
I like Gore Vidal's term for what this country has become better – the United States of Amnesia.

Dahmercracy – not exactly what any of us had in mind
His mother used to insist, "Jeffrey, I don't like your friends." Maybe he should have used the crock pot!

food boysening – new type of cuisine that makes every dish taste like berries
I love raspberries, blackberries, cherries and blueberries, but I'll pass on the linguine with purple clam sauce

hi yo Pectate – what the sidekick of the late Johnny Carson uses when things are moving too fast

Geronimantanamo – detention center where the American government held the natives in previous centuries

ax slacks – type of jeans lumberjacks use for leg protection; also, an over the counter remedy when things aren't moving along as normal for these same workers

ohnosecond – that minuscule fraction of time in which you realize that you've just made a BIG mistake

beta carrotoon – why Bugs Bunny is always healthy and smiling and has great vision

cashtration – the act of buying a house, which renders the subject financially impotent for an indefinite period – especially during late in the year 2007

diarhry – medical journal of a person with intestinal problems

Bozone – the substance surrounding stupid people that stops bright ideas from penetrating, which unfortunately, shows little sign of breaking down in the near future

decafalon – the grueling event of getting through the day consuming only things that are good for you

arachnoleptic fit – the frantic dance performed just after you've accidentally walked through a spider web

Beelzebug – Satan in the form of a mosquito, that gets into your bedroom at three in the morning and cannot be cast out

Symsophobia – fear of going shopping for clothes

Middle Yeast – using this may result in mediocre bread
*Really wild people use the **far out yeast***

liverization – movement organized to increase the iron in the diet, but not many are enthusiastic about it

perverse – the output from a destitute poet who's having a few moral dilemmas

caterpallor – the color you turn after finding half a worm in the fruit you're eating

misunderestimate – probably not a word, but if so, the double negatives cancel and it reduces to *estimate;* also, the guess that was way off is even worse

brrrpull – tug of war in Antarctica

voice maze – an answering system instituted in corporations that frees up one operator and results in complete frustration of the part of the customers
Nonetheless, "Your call is very important to us."

Looney Tunestra – drug prescribed to help with sleeping difficulties brought on by tuning in too long to the cartoon network

Macroamnesia – an island chain in the Pacific that most people have forgotten about

aerial – font used in the books, ***Flyboys*** and ***30 Seconds Over Tokyo***

times new Loman – font used in the novel, ***Death of a Salesman***

curryer – font used in the books, ***A Passage to India*** and ***The Kite Runner.***

There are more references to fonts in the chapter 11.

Corpus Day O – Caribbean offshoot of the Catholic Church that welcomes every Tom, Dick and Harry but some say was smothering

Klausvonbulowphobia – fear by dying by poison at the hands of your spouse

Iraqnaphobia – what currently is driving the administration nuts

Cathy's clone – April 1960 song by the Everly Brothers, who weren't twins

Forrest Bump – dance move in the 1970s utilized by the National Park Service

I extend my thanks to the Washington Post for the next few laughs. These came about in the year 2001.

intaxication – euphoria at getting a tax refund, which lasts until you realize that it was your money to start with

reintarnation – coming back to life as a hillbilly

foreploy – any misrepresentation about yourself for the purpose of having sex

giraffiti – vandalism spray-painted very, very high

sarchasm – the gulf between the author of sarcastic wit and the person who doesn't get it

inoculatte – to take coffee intravenously when you are running late

hipatitis – terminal coolness

osteopornosis – a degenerate disease
Whoever thought this one up should get extra credit.

Karmageddon – it's like, when everybody is sending off all these really bad vibes, right? And then, like, the earth explodes and it's like, a serious bummer

glibido – all talk and no action

Dopeler effect – the tendency of stupid ideas to seem smarter when they come at you rapidly

52

ignoranus – a person who's both stupid and . . . you can
   figure out the rest

Abramoffice – where Jack will be spending a few years with
   Bubba and Prober – he can be given a cell phone so
   he can still do business

terrortory – word used to describe a host of countries, such
   as Afghanistan, Iraq, Israel and Palestine

bye-bye-opsy – most likely the last one you'll have

Duck Cheney – good words of advice when you're hunting
   quail with the vice president

duc che nee – a new addition to the menu, not unlike Peking
   duck but with a resemblance to quail

Salvador Dali Llama – if you don't care for the art, at least it
   makes a nice pet

Tony Blair Which Project – the prime minister can't decide
   what to do next

neon conservatives – people who think they have seen the
   light

King Arthuritis – type of gout that only affects royalty

Dan Quayl – this politician has emerged with a new image,
   but still feels something is missing

   Not too many months ago, I started doing a
genealogy of my family. Some relationships still are not
exactly clear in my mind, but I think I finally got a few

53

straightened away, as some of the following should point out.

worst cousin (rhymes with first cousin) – the son or daughter of your uncle and aunt who you can't stand

a cousin once removed – relative who comes uninvited to a reunion and is escorted from the premises

a cousin twice removed – similar to a cousin once removed except he shows up in a similar situation for a second time but once more is shown the door

wurst cousin – relative who makes sausages for a living

In the late 70s I lived about forty miles north of New York City and tried to get tickets for **Saturday Night Live,** but couldn't. Instead they sent me tickets for a dress rehearsal – two hours of comedy. I saw most of the original cast, including two individuals who left us too soon.

Gilda Radner was an extremely talented woman who succumbed to cancer. She made me laugh that evening and on other numerous occasions when I saw the show on television. I particularly enjoyed her addition to the *Weekend Update* segment in the person of Emily Litella. As far as I know, the following piece was never on the show:

Emily: What's all this fuss about sandals in the church? The priests have to wear something on their feet. Since they take the vow of poverty, they probably can't afford really expensive footwear. I've never seen them wearing cordovans or spats. However, those sandals must not be too warm in December and January. That's why some of the clergy put on socks underneath – not my idea of a fashion statement. Even with the hosiery, it can't be any

54

fun in the snow. They might be advised to adopt those high boots worn by that one fellow from the Village People, except that this choice would require a bit of time lacing. Clergy are usually on the run, so this might not be a good idea and from the character of the Village People, it might send the wrong impression, although . . .

Jane: You mean scandals in the church, not sandals.

Emily: Oh, that's very different. Nevermind!

Emily: What's all this fuss about sub delays on the expressway? Perhaps that sign *Use both lanes* is meant for them. Naturally if you allow submarines on the highway, there will be delays. Those things take up three or four lanes. Besides, what are submarines doing on the freeway? Shouldn't they be in the water? I won't drive on the lake so let them stay off the highways? I have seen caravans of Army vehicles on the road and now you want to allow the Navy, too. Before long the Air Force and the Marines will want to use our highways.

Jane: Submarines aren't allowed on the freeway. The delay is due to rush hour.

Emily: Oh, that's different. *Nevermind!*

     I close the chapter with certainly not my favorite, but indeed, the most appropriate.

Déjà Moo – the feeling that you've heard this bull before

6. Brownie, you're doing a heck of a job

The United States of America seems to be going to pot. Actually, many people want to legalize marijuana so maybe it's time to do so. No matter who our leaders are, whether in the White House, the Senate or the House of Representatives, it seems like Washington, DC is suffering from an intelligence drought. Too many people across the country seem to be inheriting this dread disease. If you are not convinced, read on.

It's a wonder that anything gets passed in the nation's capital, and if it does, we now can see how these crazy laws come to be. A travel agent in Washington says she has an answer as to why this country is in trouble. Consider these examples from the experiences of others.

I had a New Hampshire Congresswoman ask for an aisle seat so that her hair wouldn't get messed up by being near the window.
The fresh air she could have gotten by leaving while the plane was in flight may have done some good – of course, not for her.

I got a call from a candidate's staffer, who wanted to go to Cape Town. I started to explain the length of the flight and the passport information, when she interrupted me with, "I'm not trying to make you look stupid, but Cape Town is in Massachusetts."
Without trying to make her look like the stupid one, I calmly explained, "Cape Cod is in Massachusetts; Cape Town is in Africa." She responded by hanging up the phone.
This staffer might wind up in Iraq by mistake – that may not be a bad thing. Maybe she was interested in the Camp Town races but didn't want to go to OTB.

57

A senior Vermont Congressman called, furious about a Florida package we did. I asked what was wrong with the vacation in Orlando. He said he was expecting an ocean-view room. I tried to explain that in Orlando it is not possible, since Orlando is in the middle of the state. He replied, "Don't lie to me. I looked on the map, and Florida is a very thin state!"

They should have given him a pair of binoculars.

I got a call from a lawmaker's wife who asked, "Is it possible to see England from Canada?"

I said, "No."

She said, "But they look so close on the map."

Actually, you can see England from Canada, but you need an awful lot of drugs.

An aide for a cabinet member once called and asked if he could rent a car in Dallas. When I pulled up the reservation, he had only a one-hour layover in Dallas. I asked why he wanted to rent a car. He said, "I heard Dallas was a big airport, and we will need a car to drive between the gates to save time."

Everything might be big in Texas, but certainly not the brains of many of the politicians and their aides.

An Illinois Congresswoman called last week. She needed to know how it was possible that her flight from Detroit left at 8:20 a.m. and got into Chicago at 8:33 a.m. I tried to explain that Michigan was an hour ahead of Illinois, but she could not understand the concept of time zones. Finally, I told her the plane went very fast, and she bought that!

I would have told her the name of the airline was Bizarro Airlines. You can fly to Europe for under $100 but you arrive there a week before you depart.

58

A New York lawmaker called and asked, "Do airlines put your physical description on your bag so they know whose luggage belongs to whom?"

I said, "No, why do you ask?"

She replied, "Well, when I checked in with the airline, they put a tag on my luggage that said FAT, and I'm overweight. I think that is very rude."

After putting her on hold for a minute while I 'looked into it' – I was actually laughing – I came back and explained the city code for Fresno, CA is FAT, and that the airline was just putting a destination tag on her luggage.

If you were a careless individual, would they put LAX on the bag?

A Senator's aide called to inquire about a trip package to Hawaii. After going over all the cost info, she asked, "Would it be cheaper to fly to California and then take the train to Hawaii?"

I would have told her Amtrak is on strike.

I just got off the phone with a freshman Congressman who asked, "How do I know which plane to get on?"

I asked him what exactly he meant, to which he replied, "I was told my flight number is 823, but none of these darn planes have numbers on them."

It's on the bottom, broccoli brain.

A lady Senator called and said, "I need to fly to Pepsi-Cola, Florida. Do I have to get on one of those little computer planes?" I asked if she meant to fly to Pensacola, Florida, on a commuter plane. She said, "Yeah, whatever."

I would have booked her on a flight to Coca-Cola, FL on Gates Airways.

A senior Senator called and had a question about the documents he needed in order to fly to China. After a lengthy discussion about passports, I reminded him that he needed a visa. "Oh, no I don't. I've been to China many times and never had to have one of those."

I double-checked, and sure enough, his stay required a visa. When I told him this he said, "Look, I've been to China four times and every time they accepted my American Express!"

I wouldn't have argued with him – maybe the Chinese will detain him permanently. Our country will be better off.

A New Mexico Congresswoman called to make reservations and said, "I want to go from Chicago to Rhino, New York." The agent was at a loss for words.

Finally, the agent said, "Are you sure that's the name of the town?"

"Yes, what flights do you have?" replied the lady.

After some searching, the agent came back with, "I'm sorry, ma'am, I've looked up every airport code in the country and can't find a Rhino anywhere."

The lady retorted, "Oh, don't be silly. Everyone knows where it is. Check your map."

The agent scoured a map of the state of New York and finally offered, "You don't mean Buffalo, do you?"

"That's it. I knew it was one of those big animals," she said.

If she's coming to my town, I'm going on vacation.

Thomas Jefferson once proposed that the United States hold annual elections on February 29.

From the results of the last two elections, February 30 may be an even better idea.

Speaking of the right to vote, here are a few tales of people who go to the ballot box, from what I'm told. It

60

doesn't mean they voted for the right candidate. The names aren't real.

While looking at a house, Melchior asked the real estate agent which direction was north because, he explained, he didn't want the sun waking him up every morning. She asked, "Does the sun rise in the north?"

When Melchior explained that the sun rises in the east – and has for some time – she shook her head and said, "Oh, I don't keep up with that stuff."

She probably never noticed.

Pat used to work in technical support for a 24/7 call center. One day she got a call from Chris, an individual who asked what hours the call center was open. She told him, "The number you dialed is open 24 hours a day, 7 days a week."

He responded, "Is that Eastern or Pacific time?" Wanting to end the call quickly, Pat said, "Uh, Pacific."

*I would have said **Southern time**.*

Dick and Harry were eating their lunch in the cafeteria, when they overheard one of the administrative assistants talking about the sunburn she got on her weekend drive to the shore. She drove down in a convertible, but "didn't think she'd get sunburned because the car was moving."

I think she wants to be the first person on the sun. I hope she takes enough sunscreen.

Rene has a lifesaving tool in her car. It's designed to cut through a seat belt if she gets trapped. She keeps it in the trunk.

It doesn't fit in her purse. They should put her in the trunk for more than one reason.

Frank and Theresa were picking up some sandwiches from the sub place last week and Theresa asked the clerk which of two sandwiches was better. The clerk didn't have an opinion but did say that the first sandwich was more expensive. Frank got a quizzical look on his face and asked, "If that's the case, why are they both listed with the same price on the menu?"

To this, the clerk responded, "I don't think we add tax to the turkey."
I didn't think poultry had a tax exemption.

Bubba and Booger were on a beer run and noticed that the cases were discounted 10%. Since it was a big party, they bought two cases. The cashier multiplied 2 times 10% and gave them a 20% discount.
The buyers thought nothing of it – they figured it was the new math.

George was hanging out with Donald when they saw a woman with a nose ring attached to an earring by a chain. George said, "Wouldn't the chain rip out every time she turned her head?" Donald explained that a person's nose and ear remain the same distance apart no matter which way the head is turned.
Apparently the same can't be said for George.

Rhonda couldn't find her luggage at the airport baggage area. So she went to the lost luggage office and told the woman there that her bags never showed up. She smiled and told the customer not to worry because she was a trained professional and Rhonda was in good hands. "Now," she asked Rhonda, "has your plane arrived yet?"
I would have told her it's been delayed, like her brain.

Some guy bought a new fridge for his house. To get rid of his old fridge, he put it in his front yard and hung a sign on it saying, "Free to good home. You want it, you take it." For three days the fridge sat there without even one person looking twice at it. He eventually decided that people were too untrusting of this deal. It looked too good to be true, so he changed the sign to read: "Fridge for sale $50." The next day someone stole it.

I'm not surprised by this turn of events. Some time ago a person in New York City supposedly gift wrapped his garbage – maybe it was a present for a friend – and put it in the back seat of his car. Someone broke into the car and stole the package. This was during the garbage strike. Presentation is everything.

I end the chapter on a religious and political note. I know; they should be separate.

The Supreme Court has ruled that there cannot be a Nativity Scene in Washington, DC this Christmas season. This isn't for any religious reason; they simply have not been able to find three wise men and a virgin in the Nation's capitol. There was no problem, however, finding enough asses to fill the stable.

Ass was used in a religious context, although I guess it could be political.

7. Trapped in the WEB

The world of technology needs a brain transplant. But don't take my word for it. Here are a few wonderful examples of the brilliant intelligence of computers and the Internet. Many of these go back to my experiences in the computer industry.

When computers arrived on the scene, they brought with them ways of getting impossible tasks done. Other jobs that may have taken hours could be accomplished in minutes. At the same time those interesting and useful machines also brought with them problems, which I will get into in another book. Computers brought a whole new language as well – and I am not alluding to Visual Basic, COBOL or C. In fact, this new vocabulary keeps evolving each day. At the same time it causes mass confusion, even to people with degrees in the subject.

A word that takes on a different meaning relative to computers is "run." Computer people say, "run the program", which simply means start the program on its way. To see how one of these programs ran, there might be a computer printout. This collection of the printouts of a group of programs may be referred to as "runs." In the old days, it may have been necessary to pick up these printouts at a remote site. If someone was supposed to go get these listings, you may have heard a secretary ask, "Did you get the runs this morning?"

The reply could have been, "Sure did. It must have been the burritos I had last night."

A computer program that is submitted to run but has not yet started is said to be "awaiting execution." A program that runs into difficulties when running because of either bad logic or bad data or both is said to "blow up." Maybe that's

65

because Joe's bill of materials explosion program was running.

You can see from these few examples that the computer business uses some very violent terms. Besides what I have already mentioned, there's "the program terminated," "the system crashed" and Frank had to "abort the program." Is it possible he did this because of computer dating?

On a serious and educational note, bad logic has been referred to as a "bug" in a program. This expression goes back to the groundbreaking days of computers. Apparently a program that was running had difficulties and after searching for the solution, an insect was discovered inside the hardware. Thus the term "bug" became the label for any difficulty a program ran into. If you wonder how such a small creature could cause so much havoc, consider the cockroach. If you have any electronic equipment and this fellow gets inside, say goodbye to that machine. It will never work again. The cockroach crawls about the insides of the unit and leaves a residue from his body that turns the equipment into junk.

When I was working at Nestle Foods in White Plains, we figured that you had to have some fun from time to time. One day a friend of mine happened to come upon a member of the insect world, whose life he promptly snuffed out. He then took the remains and gently placed it inside one of our computer listings. A few of us then proceeded to our supervisor's office and told him that we found the bug in the program that was troubling us for some time. Maybe, we should have done this on a day when Hugo was in a better mood. However, when we left him, I'm sure he had a good laugh and probably related this incident more than I have.

A mainframe computer is nothing more than a really large computer that cost millions of dollars, such as an IBM model. When I worked on this type of system and it had major problems, it was necessary to "re-start" the monster and this was done in one of two ways: either a cold start or a warm start. A cold start had to do with starting all over, whereas a warm start entailed restarting, although not from the very beginning. That's the best way I can describe it. I have heard people on occasion talking about the need to cold start or warm start the computer when all I wanted to add was, "Why not do a lukewarm start?"

The term PC obviously refers to personal computers in this discussion. I have other meanings for what those two letters represent and you can find them a few paragraphs down as well as in other books of mine. Over the years and it still applies today, people who bought PCs have gotten obsessed with their new tool of technology. Some have spent hour after hour in front of the machine and others have been logged on to the Internet for days on end. It has even gotten to the point where family or friends have to make a call to PC anonymous. This scenario has caused the breakup of some families and some bad feelings. In light of this situation, perhaps that piece of equipment should be called an "impersonal computer."

I was investigating a program one time when I saw a description at the top that said, "This program sweeps through the data base." Actually, as I was doing this, it was only two nights before Halloween. We should be on the alert for witches with brooms. They could help, here.

The early days of computers found an operator watching his console to monitor what was going on in the machine. The console would tell when a job started and finished as well as when it crapped out – that may not have been the term used, but I think you get the idea. The early consoles were nothing more than fancy typewriters that produced one line of print after the other.

We still have those consoles today but they are more likely to have a screen, such as a CRT or cathode ray tube. They still produce lines of information, some of which I don't understand. On one job, I could simulate a console to peek at jobs as they ran. One day the console indicated that someone was creating a job that was producing numerous lines of print. It was over a million lines and the program was still running and sure to create more. A short time later I noticed the following message on the console:

LOGGING IN EFFECT

I thought to myself, is someone chopping down trees? Of course they were. They needed paper for all the printout of that aforementioned job.

I heard an associate say that he had another wave of programs. And I thought, "Oh no, not the wave!" I assumed it was passé. However, I did see a message on the console, which might be related. It said:

COMPUTER IS DRAINED

Maybe there was a flood in the computer room. I think I know the cause. Earlier I also heard my boss mention to someone, "We'll meet and flush out the problems." I was going to ask if they were planning to meet in the john but then I knew where the meeting was.

This last message on the console I swear I did not make up. It said:

SUBMITTED FOR BUNDLING TRIGGER

I wonder if Dale Evans or any of the Rogers' children know about this.

I spent about two months on a contract assignment at Sea World in Orlando, Florida. We developed some software for the corporation on a system of PCs. The language we used for the application was COBOL but considering the company maybe it should have been written in the "C" language.

I created a new web site and tried to load it on June 20, 2005. While attempting to do that, I received the message, "Invalid password or ID." My old logon and password didn't work because the web host assigned a new combination. I emailed them, asking for the actual ID and password and shortly afterwards got the reply that she would mail it to an old email address that they had on file for me. But that was a full mailbox and couldn't accept any messages. I had to email back the person to tell them that I wouldn't get what she sent at my old email address. So why did she send me the message in the first place to the right address and then offer to send the password elsewhere. Why couldn't she have sent the ID and password in the first place? *"Beam me up, Scotty, there's no intelligence on this planet."*

Here's something that everyone suffers through. You have a file that you want to delete, so you go through the procedure to get rid of it by pressing the delete key. You might think that the file is now removed, but it's not, as you need to answer the question, "Are you sure?" When you hit "Yes," another question arises, "Are you really sure?" Entering "Yes" should now result in the file being gone, but it has only been moved to a recycle bin. It's unfortunate that those who came up with this procedure weren't tossed into the garbage! However, there will be other occasions in which you have a file one day and the next day it is mysteriously gone from the galaxy, never ever to be found again! *What we really need is a method to delete some of the people who designed this software.*

Usually to sign off a PC (Piece of Crap), you have to go to "start" and then press "log off" and then just for good measure, press "turn off." I guess they want to make sure you weren't kidding about logging off. I was online one day when all of a sudden not only was I logged off the Internet, I was also logged out of my PC (Positively Crud). I didn't even have to click anything. I wish I could log off that fast every day. Days later, I wound up clicking "start," then I got a different screen than usual and then I clicked "log off."
Who designed this PC (Pain in the Crotch)?

On April 12, 2005, I changed my email address because of huge amounts of spam, most of it pornography. The provider I used was the same because of some of the features it had. However, I sent two bulk emails to notify people of this change, and the first one was rejected because there were too many recipients. I cut down the list and got around that problem. I sent another bulk mailing for the same purpose but was worried that maybe I had too many people listed in the "to" field. Fortunately, the email went through. I then proceeded to send another email with less recipients and it failed. I cut the list in half and was successful. I then tried to send the email to those who I had left off and I got the messages:
You have reached your message sending limit for the hour. This limit will increase as you continue to use Yahoo! Mail. This limit is in place to prevent abuse of our system.
Apparently their idea didn't work too well on my old email address. I guess you know why this provider is called "Yahoo."

To further illustrate that the designers of the software for my email provider are a bunch of Yahoos, let me relate what happened on July 13, 2005. I was looking at my email when suddenly I got bounced and had to log on again. When

70

I tried to do that by entering my ID and password, I was denied access. I tried a few times but was not successful. By the way, I entered it correctly. Finally I clicked on the link which said, "If you are not so and so, click here," even though that was my ID. I then got a slightly different logon screen, which I used to get back on.
Some of these software people must be smoking oakum.

I received a letter in May 2005 from Jesse, a friend of mine who isn't very thrilled with computers. He worked with me at Nestle Foods in White Plains years ago in our computer business lives. Unfortunately, he can't avoid using a PC. So far, he does know how to turn it on. I'm a bit further on but still am confused by the admonition, "Hit any key." I've been looking on my keyboard, but I can't find the "any" key. Anyway, he did mention that he does check his email every third month.
Some people with email don't come close to checking it that often.

On Friday, March 3, 2006, I joined two friends for dinner at Shepherd's, a restaurant close to my house. One of the guys called me in the afternoon after sending me an email, asking me to call him. After looking at the electronic correspondence, I noticed the date on it – July 25, 2005. Huh?
I wonder if he has a time machine.

I'm not thrilled with nor do I use PowerPoint unless I really have to. That's because I don't get involved with software that doesn't work. A few people have mentioned to me that they were at PowerPoint presentations and in many cases there were difficulties. I sat through similar experiences at meetings. Why is there a need to use such a tool when it only seems to emphasize our TV mentality? That term is an oxymoron, by the way. I think I figured out where the name of the software being discussed originated. The inventor was working with it and said, "Oh, oh, there's no power, so what's the point?

The May 29, 2005 issue of Parade magazine described a new type of alarm clock, called the "clocky." After it sounds and the snooze button is pushed, it rolls off the nightstand and around the room. Once it rings again, the drowsy person needs to look for it and thus will be awake for the day's activities. Whoever designed this device wasn't using his or her brain. This product could be greatly enhanced by having it explode when the snooze button is pressed. This would accomplish a few things: the person in the room would most likely arise but the company producing the "clocky" would now have another sale and more profits. A taxi would get some business driving the victim to the hospital and a furniture store would have a chance to sell some furniture to the inhabitant of the blasted bedroom. There's a good chance that another hospital bed would be occupied for a few days and some type of construction firm would get a call for work rebuilding the bedroom. Many people stand to profit from this improvement. I'm surprised that the makers of this clock didn't think of all this. After all, they are scientists at MIT.

Perhaps MIT stands for Missing Intelligent Techniques.

Another example of the brilliance of those who design web pages had to do with the book I wrote in 2005, *for seeing eye dogs only*. That is not a mistake; the words are in lowercase. If you haven't read the book, it's a humorous look at missing intelligence, of which the book you are reading is sort of a sequel. Another book in this same vein is **Non Campus Mentis** by Anders Henricksson. It's a hysterical look at history through the eyes of college students who were snoozing during the lecture. But getting back to my book, when I got to AMAZON.COM and entered the title, the cover of my book appeared and a few lines down came the following:

Customers interested in For Seeing Eye Dogs Only may also be interested in
Sponsored Links (<u>What's this?</u>) <u>Feedback</u>
<u>GuidingEyes for the Blind</u>
Premier Non-profit Guide Dog School needs your support!
<u>http://www.guidingeyes.org</u>
<u>The **Seeing Eye**</u>
Find out how **Seeing Eye dogs** enrich the lives of blind people.
<u>www.seeingeye.org</u>
If you've read my book, you will realize that only indirectly is it about the blind. It's true that it deals with instances where it seems that people can't see very clearly. However, that is not because they are blind. Amazon's suggestions are another example of missing intelligence.

Staying with that same web company, I ordered a music CD in August 2005 but there was difficulty in obtaining it. It seems the warehouse was out of stock. Thus I was notified that it was to be shipped no earlier than September 21. On September 24th, I got an email that basically stated that there was a delay with the item. They apologized for the inconvenience and asked me to approve the delay so they could continue processing. Obviously I knew there was a delay. I had been waiting for the CD for over a month. I ordered the music because I wanted it and I didn't approve of any delay but I had already accepted that situation for some time. Why then would I want to cancel the order? Wouldn't it make more sense to ask me to cancel the order and if I didn't, it meant I still wanted the CD? It gets worse. I went to the web site to "approve the delay," which I did. About a week later I got an email saying my order was

73

cancelled because I didn't take the necessary action. If they don't want my business, I will go elsewhere. That's what America is all about.

Every so often while on the Internet, I get the message "this document contains no data." Many times messages that you see are really quite misleading.
I think what they really mean is that the mind of the designer of this software is empty.

Three words that illustrate only too clearly that technology has run amok are, "Our records show." In March 2005, I bought a new car. In the year that followed, I have been receiving notices, all irresponsible, from either the corporation that makes this vehicle or from the dealer where I purchased it. One such correspondence reached me on January 18, 2006. Keep in mind that at this point I had not yet owned the car for one year, and I had reduced the miles I drive considerably since retiring. It said, "Our records show that your car is overdue for the following dealer recommended maintenance: *51,000 oil change service.* I doubt that the note indicated I should have 51,000 oil changes but rather it implied that my car's odometer had registered that many miles.
Perhaps this company needs a better service for keeping their records.

I'm sure you have experienced the time limit scenario while either dialing a phone number or in front of the ATM. If you haven't, it goes something like this. While depositing or withdrawing money from the bank, the system gives you time to enter your password as well as the amount of the transaction. Similarly, if you use a long distance provider and need to enter an 800 number as well as a long password – the card identification – you are given time as well to put in the number of the party you are trying to reach. In either case, if you don't press the keys fast enough, you might get a message asking if you need more time. It might get worse. When I did this thing with the phone, apparently I didn't enter the number fast enough because I heard the message, "That number is not valid," and I was finished. In my situation, the system allowed not much more than a second between the numbers entered, if that much. Who was the brilliant designer of this software?

I also want to know why the card id has to be twelve digits. Does this phone company really anticipate one day having almost one trillion customers? If so, they better reconsider taking them all on. The computer won't be able to handle one trillion accounts without crashing. The examples in this chapter should convince you of this.

One day I needed to print out the beginning of the book I was writing, but I didn't need the first page. Page 0 was the dedication page, so I thought I would start and print pages one to ten. That's a total of ten (10) pages. I'd have to figure out later how to print the Table of Contents, which was on page ii. After printing was complete, I wound up with twelve (12) pages. I wanted 10, but I got 12. I guess computers don't follow ordinary rules of mathematics.

More recently I wanted to print out in reverse order pages 51 through 75 of a book I am writing. On the panel that allows you to do this selection, I entered 75-51, which should have given me what I needed. Instead pages 73, 74, 75 and 48 were printed. I wish I made this story up.

Spellchecker is another great tool if you want a few laughs. To use it in WORD, click on "Tools" and then "Spelling and Grammar." Even if you have checked your document, give it a go and you may wind up with a smile on your face.

A few years ago, when I worked a contract at Citigroup in Rochester, I wound up documenting a project in which I was involved. One of the people who I worked with was Paul Spagnoli, who was very cooperative and answered any question I had. I included his name in the write-up I did on the project and when I finished, I cranked up spellchecker. This wonderful piece of software flagged his name. However, it did give a suggestion for an alternative – something it usually does. It offered, *spittoon!*
The expression "garbage in, garbage out" is older than the hills. I suggest "Good software was never produced by someone with the intelligence of a 'Frisbee.'"

On a lighter note, I got an email recently on Elementronics. I haven't verified this with any scientists but I believe it's true.

The heaviest element known to science is *managerium*. This element has no protons or electrons, but has a nucleus composed of one neutron, two vice-neutrons, five junior vice-neutrons, twenty-five assistant vice-neutrons, and 125 junior assistant vice-neutrons all going round in circles. Managerium has a half-life of three years, at which time it does not decay but institutes a series of reviews leading to reorganization. Its molecules are held together by means of the exchange of tiny particles known as morons.

My friend Helene called with a PC problem. It seems she lost the use of her mouse. I made a few suggestions but that didn't help her. I only wished her good luck. As a friend of mine said once when dealing with problems of the computer, "The possibilities are endless."
Once I hung up the phone, it came to me that her mouse died – it got cancer from laboratory testing.

76

8. Medical brilliance

If this chapter doesn't clear up why I chose **wake up – it's time for your sleeping pill** as the title for this book, nothing will. Unfortunately, the profession doesn't have a monopoly on missing intelligence. Much of what follows was collected from people who love to email. With each passing day my email evolves into *correspondunce*, but every so often I do get some gems. I can't vouch for the authenticity of these events – not all health related – but they sure are worth a laugh. They are examples of why evolution needs more work.

They say you should never represent yourself at a trial and here's one example why. Springfield, Massachusetts was the scene in April 2005 for Thomas B. Dazzled and his questionable law practice. He was convicted but tried to appeal the decision by acting as his own lawyer. He then asked for his conviction to be overturned since his lawyer was incompetent.
As ridiculous as this was, he appears to not be alone in brain deficiencies as the decision is still pending.

The following are all replies that women from Dallas, Texas have written on Child Support Agency forms in the section for listing "father's details." It could be put another way – "Who's your Daddy?" These are supposedly genuine excerpts from the forms.

Regarding the identity of the father of my twins, child A was fathered by Jim Munson. I am unsure as to the identity of the father of child B, but I believe that he was conceived on the same night.

I am unsure, as to the identity of the father of my child as I was being sick out of a window when taken unexpectedly from behind. I can provide you with a list of names of men that I think were at the party if this helps.

I do not know the name of the father of my little girl. She was conceived at a party at 3600 Grand Avenue where I had unprotected sex with a man I met that night. I do remember that the sex was so good that I fainted. If you do manage to track down the father, can you send me his phone number? Thanks.

I don't know the identity of the father of my daughter. He drives a BMW that now has a hole made by my stiletto in one of the door panels. Perhaps you can contact BMW service stations in this area and see if he's had it replaced.

I have never had sex with a man. I am still a Virginian. I am awaiting a letter from the Pope confirming that my son's conception was ejaculate and that he is the Saver risen again.
Perhaps CSI: DC could help her – it's really close.

I cannot tell you the name of child A's dad as he informs me that to do so would blow his cover and that would have cataclysmic implications for the economy. I am torn between doing right by you and right by the country. Please advise.
Maybe he's in the administration. I don't think he's selling shoes.

Peter Smith is the father of child A. If you do catch up with him, can you ask him what he did with my AC / DC CDs? Child B who was also borned at the same time. Well, I don't have clue.
I heard she changed her story a lot.

From the dates it seems that my daughter was conceived at Disney World; maybe it really is the Magic Kingdom.
I bet her partner was Houdini.

So much about that night is a blur. The only thing that I remember for sure is Delia Smith did a program about eggs earlier in the evening. If I had stayed in and watched more TV rather than going to the party at 146 Miller Drive, mine might have remained unfertilized.
It seems the yoke is on her.

I am unsure as to the identity of the father of my baby, after all, like when you eat a can of beans you can't be sure which one made you fart.
I thought flatulence was a group thing rather than a single bean. Talk about bad analogies.

Someone sent the next set of tales from the medical profession along with the names of the doctors. I have left out the names of the physicians for a variety of reasons – they really add nothing to the story. From reading them, you may realize why you should avoid hospitals and doctors' offices as much as possible.

A man ran into the ER yelling, "My wife's going to have her baby in the cab!" I grabbed my stuff, rushed out to the cab, lifted the lady's dress, and began to take off her underwear. Suddenly I noticed that there were several cabs – I was in the wrong one.

One day I had to be the bearer of bad news when I told a wife that her husband had died of a massive myocardial infarct. Not more than five minutes later, I heard her reporting to the rest of the family that he had died of a "massive internal fart."

79

I was performing a complete physical, including the visual acuity test. I placed the patient twenty feet from the chart and began, "Cover your right eye with your hand." He read the 20/20 line perfectly. "Now your left." Again, a flawless read. "Now both," I requested. There was silence. He couldn't even read the large E on the top line. I turned and discovered he was doing exactly what I had asked; he was standing there with both his eyes covered. I was laughing too hard to finish the exam.

During a patient's two-week follow-up appointment with his cardiologist, he informed me, his doctor, that he was having trouble with one of his medications. I asked, "Which one?"
"The patch. The nurse told me to put on a new one every six hours and now I'm running out of places to put it!" I had him quickly undress and discovered the man had over fifty patches on his body! Now, the instructions include removal of the old patch before applying a new one.
I wonder if he considered looking for a place on his wife's body.

While acquainting myself with a new elderly patient, I asked, "How long have you been bedridden?"
After a look of complete confusion she answered, "Why, not for about twenty years – when my husband was alive."

I was caring for a woman and asked, "So how's your breakfast this morning?"
"It's very good, except for the Kentucky Jelly. I can't seem to get used to the taste," the patient replied. I asked to see the jelly and the woman produced a foil packet labeled "KY Jelly."

A new, young MD doing his residency in OB was quite embarrassed performing female pelvic exams. To cover his embarrassment he had unconsciously formed a habit of whistling softly. The middle-aged lady upon whom he was performing this exam suddenly burst out laughing and further embarrassed him. He looked up from his work and sheepishly said, "I'm sorry. Was I tickling you?"

She replied, "No doctor, but you're whistling, 'I wish I was an Oscar Mayer wiener.'"

In this case the doctor didn't supply his name. I wouldn't have either.

Nurses and doctors have way too much paperwork. From reading some of the following actual writings from hospital charts, you should be convinced that most of them are overworked.

The patient refused autopsy.
He thought it was an imposition.

The patient has no previous history of suicides.
There's a first time for everything.

Patient has left white blood cells at another hospital.
He probably changed health care providers.

Note: patient here recovering from forehead cut. Patient became very angry when given an enema by mistake.
Luckily, they took the knife away.

Patient has chest pain if she lies on her left side for over a year.
She should change hospitals.

Discharge status: Alive but without permission.
This is one tough hospital. Please don't send me there.

81

On the second day the knee was better, and on the third day it disappeared.
Fortunately, the patient didn't have heart surgery.

The patient is tearful and crying constantly. She also appears to be depressed.
At least she still has her knee.

The patient has been depressed since she began seeing me in 1993.
Maybe the health care profession isn't for him – he should try shipbuilding.

Healthy appearing, decrepit 69-year old male, mentally alert but forgetful.

Patient had waffles for breakfast and anorexia for lunch.
I wonder who does the cooking.

She is numb from her toes down.
She may have to be amputated from the neck down.

While in ER, she was examined, x-rated and sent home.
Maybe the patient is related to Buck Naked.

The skin was moist and dry.
What did they expect after giving her dry ice to drink.

Occasional, constant, infrequent headaches.
This seems to be an oxymoronic pleonasm.

Patient was alert and unresponsive.
Bring some food and see if that makes a difference.

Rectal examination revealed a normal size thyroid.
I wonder what they were treating.

She stated that she had been constipated for most of her life, until she got a divorce.
Don't tell the drug companies about this breakthrough.

The lab test indicated abnormal lover function.
Things should improve around Valentine's Day.

I saw your patient today, who is still under our car for physical therapy.
Did he have a broken exhaust system?

Skin: somewhat pale but present.
That's a great sign.

Patient has two teenage children, but no other abnormalities.
What are the kids' names – Cancer and Throb?

Examination of genitalia reveals that he is circus sized.
So that's why all the nurses were hanging around the patient.

The following are notes written by parents for their children for some reason or other – mostly sickness.

Please excuse Gloria from Jim today? She is administrating.
Can't she find anyone better than Jim?

Please excuse Lisa for being absent she was sick and I had her shot.
Lisa should have hid the bullets beforehand.

83

My son is under a doctor's care and should not take PE today. Please execute him.
Won't that prevent the school from getting government funding?

Dear school: Please ecsc's John being absent on Jan. 28, 29, 30, 31, 32 and also 33.
What about the 34th and 35th? Now you know why they sent John to school.

Please excuse Roland from P.E. for a few days. Yesterday he fell out of a tree and misplaced his hip.
He must have rolled out of the tree. Was he raking leaves? I hope he finds it soon.

John has been absent because he had two teeth taken out of his face.
He would have had a lot less pain if they were taken out of Neutron's face.

Carlos was absent yesterday because he was playing football. He was hurt in the growing part.
It won't be growing for a while.

Megan could not come to school today because she has been bothered by very close veins.
I didn't think senior citizens needed their parents to write excuses for them.

Please excuse Ray Friday from school. He has very loose vowels.
I don't want to hear about his consonants. Can his friends hang around him?

Please excuse Pedro from being absent yesterday. He had (diahre, dyrea, direathe,) – oh nevermind that, the &%$#s.
He's probably hanging around Ray too much.

Chris will not be in school cus he has an acre in his side.
That must be painful. I'm glad it's him and not me.

Please excuse Tommy for being absent yesterday. He had diarrhea, and his boots leak.
In his case, it's good to know about the boots.

Irving was absent yesterday because he missed his bust.
At least he won't be spending any time in jail.

I kept Billie home because she had to go Christmas shopping because I don't know what size she wear.
Buy something she'll grow into.

Please excuse Jennifer for missing school yesterday. We forgot to get the Sunday paper off the porch, and when we found it Monday, we thought it was Sunday.
They're lucky the dog didn't eat the paper.

Sally won't be in school a week from Friday. We have to attend her funeral.
What some people won't do to get out of class. I hope they invited her teacher to the breakfast afterwards.

My daughter was absent yesterday because she was tired. She spent a weekend with the Marines.
It doesn't sound like she was faithful.

Please excuse Jason for being absent yesterday. He had a cold and could not breed well.
She used the excuse about his being in a movie last week.

Please excuse Mary for being absent yesterday. She was in bed with gramps.
I thought he went to Florida with Grandma.

Gloria was absent yesterday as she was having a gangover.
Didn't the Marines have another engagement?

Please excuse Brenda. She has been sick and under the doctor.
Someone said he needed more practice.

Maryann was absent December 11-16, because she had a fever, sore throat, headache and upset stomach. Her sister also was sick, fever and sore throat, her brother had a low grade fever and ached all over. I wasn't the best either, sore throat and fever. There must be something going around, her father even got hot last night.
This explains the son's bad marks and it sounds like this home needs a quarantine.

I really don't care for bathroom humor even though I roared over George Carlin's bit on defecation, especially the airline stuff. I thought about not including this, but then I got inspired and figured I had to relate what I went through with the medical profession. I will try to give the events that occurred some class. It's a long tale of frustration, illogic and missing intelligence, so you may want to get a beer. Also, put on your boots – you are going to need them, as you will see.

The el toro crappo incident

In March 2006, I needed to get some routine medical testing done. There's the blood work, urine test and one other part called hemoccult screening. From the title of that last test, I should have known that I was cursed. I got through the first two of three parts in the lab and took the kit home. It sounded like I had to assemble something, which I didn't feel like doing.

Once I got to read over the material, I found that I had to fast from certain types of food before proceeding. I had plenty of food choices but I had to have a seventy-two hour period in which I did not eat red meat, fresh fruits or fresh vegetables. I also couldn't have more than 250 mg of vitamin C. I made this discovery after breakfast on Tuesday and realized that I had to start counting from the previous evening's dinner. This meant that I had the pleasure of capturing the required samples just before dinner on Thursday evening, which I did.

The next day – which if you are keeping track is Friday – I drove the precious stuff over to the lab but was informed that I needed three specimens. Since I followed my grasping in the toilet bowl shortly thereafter with ingesting some raw vegetables as well as swallowing 1000 mg of C, I figured I just might have to start over with my limited fast. I asked at the lab and was advised to call my family doctor, who had sent me to the lab in the first place. The vitamin C was fine, I was told, but the vegetables were a problem. I complained about the specific instructions I was given on a piece of paper, which did not request three helpings, but my complaints went for naught. However, I was informed that there was another option, something called "The ensure test." I thought that was a liquid for old people.

I was told that the restrictions before this test were not as stringent as the triple trapping tryst, but I wondered why I wasn't given that option originally. I was told to contact the lab, which I did, but they required a new script from my doctor. At this point, I felt like I was in the medical *Twilight Zone*, but nonetheless called the doctor's office and asked them to fax over the script to the lab. This was after two in the afternoon and I gave them until three o'clock to get the material over. At three, I called the lab but they hadn't gotten the fax yet. I asked Ecstasy – not her real name – how long she would be there and she mentioned 4:30 pm. I decided I needed a break and went out for a walk.

While getting some much needed exercise, I figured I had two choices: I could continue the triple specimen ensnarement or go for the *ensure* option and be sure. I also thought of a turd alternative. Instead of doing either test, which involved sitting on the throne, having a movement, fishing and who knows what else, why not just get a bucket, put some water into it and sit on it until the desired results ensue – that sounds similar to *ensure*, without the "r." Of course, this procedure might take three days, which I thought might be an imposition. In any case, I had to cover the bucket with plastic wrap and drive it carefully over to the lab, telling them to help themselves and send whatever they didn't want to my doctor. If they wanted more, they should let me know. I could make arrangements.

I also came up with another possibility. On the Ellicott Creek Trailway, I see plenty of dogs as well as numerous Canada Geese flying overhead. The dogs don't fly. Each of these animals from time to time will leave souvenirs on the path – even though most people don't desire these offerings. Why shouldn't I use one of these droppings from those beautiful creatures of the country that borders on our north? This is something I really care to do. It can be accomplished by bringing along a plastic bag with some device to put a sample into that very bag and then the rest of the process can be finished at home. The other option is to bring the Ensure kit on my journey, do the capturing right there, finish the task – remembering to do the proper labeling

88

– and then drop off the stamped enveloped into a nearby mailbox.

There could be a problem with this choice. It probably means I am not done with the Ensure requirement. Moreover, the lab or my doctor might mention to me that the test showed that I wasn't an American citizen and that the results indicated that I had the unusual capability of being able to fly.

I didn't choose the last few alternatives, though. When I returned home, there was a message from the doctor's staff that I could pick up the kit at the office – it didn't seem like they were going to fax any script for me. I thought about going to pick up this kit so I called the office to ask what time they closed. I got the answering service so I knew I'd have to wait until Monday. I did have another alternative since it wasn't quite 4:30, so I called the lab. Unfortunately, I got their answering machine.

I realize that this is becoming an epic – by the way that is the name of some kind of health care drug program – but I warned you about the boots and I still haven't done my duty. I did call the lab on Saturday but only got the answering machine again. However, I figured that all this stuff would have to wait.

On Monday, I called the lab and once again didn't talk to anyone. I patiently waited through the endless diatribe on the machine and eventually was told that I had two messages – which I listened to. Eventually, I was told that the phone call was over. I submitted and called the doctor's office and was told that the fax was never sent, as I figured and as I requested. I was told the office would be open until 5:30, so I drove over and picked up the Insure kit – I spelled it wrong before. Spellchecker missed it as well. The official name of this doodad – pun intended – is **F**ecal **I**mmunochemical **T**est. I thought the acronym was certainly appropriate, in my case.

89

I can say this about the kit, the office was right. There were no food restrictions, the effort on my part would be much easier and the directions stated that eating fruits and vegetables could actually increase test accuracy. With the materials I got, I also found two paint brushes and figured it wouldn't be as easy as I thought. Fortunately, no art was required and an addressed envelope with postage was included. Usually what I get in the mail is crap. A day later, I returned the favor and the lab got my present shortly thereafter. I tossed my trial run – no pun intended – into the trash. This whole incident only shows why some medical care people use the word "practice!"

One important thing for each of us is a living will. You may not want this one, but there are plenty of alternatives. Talk to your attorney.

A man and his wife were sitting in the living room and he said to her, "Just so you know, I never want to live in a vegetative state, dependent on some machine and fluids from a bottle. If that ever happens, just pull the plug." His wife got up, unplugged the TV and threw out all of his beer.

9. That's what the sign said

Signs can be found everywhere – along the highways, on products, on the back of a package of food, as well as at places of business. You can't avoid them and some are really funny.

No long ago while on my way home, I passed the Buffalo International Airport and saw a sign on Genesee Street. It said, **Low flying planes**. It seems a bit redundant. We can't blame the sign painters on this one – they were just doing their job. If I am walking in the area, should I duck my head?
Maybe someone should talk to the pilots.

While waiting in line at the bank that I have the privilege of using, I saw the following signs: **Get excited about pumping gas**, and **Get excited about buying paper towels**. I always felt that if you wanted intelligence, the last place you should look is at a bank. Is it me, or is the advertising world running out of ideas? I presented the clerk with a deposit slip with the amount that added up to the sum of the two twenties I handed her plus three small checks. She asked if I wanted it all put in, whatever that means. I should have said I wanted $20 back. I had to excuse her. She's a blond!
I'm happy to report that these advertisements or whatever they were are gone. One person can make a difference.

I saw an ad for a **reciprocating saw** in the newspaper. *Perhaps someone did this tool some harm.*

There's a sign in Williamsville near my house for the **Main-Transit Fire Department**.
It's on neither Main Street nor Transit Road but rather on Sheridan Drive.

While driving on Maple in the town of Williamsville, I saw a sign on the back window of a van that said, **duplicating consultants**.
Aren't there enough consultants already? Do they use a Xerox machine in this process?

On a trip down south during the fall of 2005, I saw the sign, **Urgent message when flashing**. On a trip a few years before that, it was flashing.
Maybe it wasn't flashing this time because I told a lot less people about this trip. You'll have to read my previous book, for seeing eye dogs only, to fully understand this.

I also saw a sign that said, **Starbucks...open 24 hours**.
You'll be awake for twenty-four hours if you stop there too many times.

Pennsylvania has this sign: **Buckle up next million miles**.
But I wasn't going that far.

In Maryland, one of the roads has an unusual name. It's called the **Sam Eig Highway**. They must have run out of letters for the signs or at least there was a shortage of consonants. They should check with Vanna.
Why isn't there a John Wilkes Booth Boulevard, Benedict Arnold Ally or a Lee Harvey Oswald Lane?

I saw this sign while I was logged on to the Internet. It said, **Help her find her match**.
Why, is she trying to light the barbecue?

You may see this ad in the future: **Sign up for your free plutonium Visa Card**.
I'm happy with my uranium card.

92

On many trips I have seen the sign, ***Local tourist information.***
I didn't think local people did the tourist thing in their home town.

I received a mailing from my credit card company that said, "Did you know that you're free to choose what day your payment is due?"
I really wanted to call and tell them my choice was December 31, 2099. This is probably another example of "correspondunce."

On my way into the supermarket I happened to see a vanity license plate that read, ***BORSOX.*** I assume it has to do with the Boston Red Sox and I think it is quite appropriate. Watching them or any other major league baseball team play can be just that – boring. Speaking of that team, there's more in the chapter that follows.

I was driving on the road and a few cars in front of me, I saw a truck that had ***M. S. Carriers*** written on the back. I hope that's not what I think it transports.
Think degrees, such as BS, MS, and PhD – Piled Higher and Deeper.

Perhaps this next observation should have been in Chapter 6. In fact it is related to that chapter title. I am sure you have seen the question, *"What can Brown do for you?"*
As is all too obvious from the disaster in New Orleans after Hurricane Katrina, he didn't do much and certainly not enough.

In most cases, you can't tell a book by the cover. I do believe you can sell a book by the cover and I might add, the title. They can both make a difference. There is a book out

entitled, ***How to Cook Everything***, which I have no intention of buying.
I certainly have no desire to cook an old shoe, a telemarketer or an aardvark. But that's me.

Grocery stores have ads that cause you to think as well. I saw an advertisement for **shark steaks – wild caught**.
That's reassuring. Now I know they didn't get them from the zoo.
Another ad I saw mentioned something called **sleeved lettuce**.
In this case, I know a head is involved, but I didn't think arms were.

I watched the movie ***Good Night, and Good Luck*** and thought it was inspiring, powerful and one of my favorite all time movies. Just before the flick began, I saw the rating for it, which I really don't recall but I saw that the movie had ***mild thematic elements***. According to the Merriam-Webster dictionary, "thematic" refers to the topic of discourse or melodic subject. As far as I can tell, every movie has a subject and certainly music will be present – I see no reason to throw out those three words while rating it. *Perhaps this "thematic" thing has varying degrees, just like salsa – mild, medium and hot. I guess the last designation applies to movies made in South America.*
The rating also mentioned ***brief language***.
Before seeing the production, I figured that those words meant that there would be a great deal of discussion about underwear or else there would be all one-syllable words. After viewing the Clooney work, I saw neither undergarments or discussion of same, nor discourse that utilized simple words.

A friend and I headed over for lunch after he went through a colonoscopy. We walked in the door and waited to be seated but wound up standing around. Finally, we selected a table and sat down. My companion really didn't want to be standing at this point – if you've had this procedure, you know what I mean. A hostess came by and told us that we couldn't sit at that table and directed us to another section. After looking over the menu, it was apparent that it was limited, lunch wise. I'm sure the restaurant had a single all-purpose menu, rather than a separate one for dinner.

We decided on what to order and I handed the waitress a discount coupon for a free lunch. However, she said that it was invalid since we ordered dinner entrees. I don't know about you, but I think the difference between lunch and dinner has to do with the time you eat as opposed to what you eat. It was no big deal as eventually I used an Entertainment card for a free dinner. When we were done, we agreed that the food was quite good.

You've heard of the soup Nazi and I have been to restaurants that I am sure are owned by his relatives as well as encountered others of his family in different endeavors. You just can't escape these people – they're really annoying but they give me a lot of material. But getting back to lunch, – or was it dinner? – by her coupon denial, the server saved us money and kept it out of the cash register. Her tip wasn't any larger and I'm sure anyone who went through what we did may have left an even smaller tip. What is wrong with the way some businesses treat their customers?

I wrote about this before in my 2005 book on intelligence follies, but it seems people haven't caught on to my suggestion. I still keep seeing the two words, *free gift*. The phrase doesn't seem to be going away. There's no such thing as a free lunch and certainly no *free gift*, for in some way, you'll have to pay. On the other hand, doesn't one give a gift, expecting nothing in return?

Not long ago I tried to get some free software. I decided against it because in the process I would have had to buy ten

CDs through some music club and would need to contribute fifty pints of blood for the revolution. However, there was good news as I could do that over time. Actually, it wasn't that bad as the last requirement I made up, but the music deal was required.

I saw an email that had for its title, **Serious Christian Singles**.
Needless to say, I didn't respond since I want to be with people who have a good sense of humor and don't mind laughing. This must be a group of practicing Catholics. They should work more on smiling.

The day after I saw the above gem, I got an email that said, **Meet real, honest singles in your area**.
Is there actually an opportunity to meet people who are dishonest? I want to meet women who aren't real – that way I don't have to pay for their dinner or worry about them filling up my inbox.

On my way home from my daily walk, I saw these words on the St. James Church changing billboard: **Last Supper Re-enactment**.
I don't believe this is with the original cast.

In a previous book, I mentioned my involvement in a lawsuit as a plaintiff – for a possible payoff of $45 – and the details aren't important. The folder with the information had the following words:
This page intentionally left blank.
Those five words were the beginning of the title of the book I had published in late 2007. People are still abusing the phrase. In early June 2008, I was sent a brochure which had something written on the back while the page before was completely blank. The two pages preceding it each had five words, and only those five – the phrase listed above. I would

have preferred no writing on those three pages or at least the words, **this page intentionally left blank** *on the trio – annoying to me, but at least, consistent.*

One of the supermarkets where I shop had the sign: **Sidewalk chalk bubblegum.**
I guess you can write on the pavement and then lick it off and chew the gum.

One of the supermarkets in Buffalo had an ad for **adult cereal.**
You wouldn't believe what the Rice Krispies were doing.

On the day following the election in November 2006, C-Span provided percentages for the races along with the fact that 116% of the vote had been reported.
At this point, they should be able to project a winner. Shouldn't they wait for more votes to come in?

I saw a sign that said, **Fed Ex Express.**
Doesn't this really translate to Federal Express Express? This is the only shipping method used by Mary Hartman, Mary Hartman.

While on the road one day I saw a truck with **Integrity Distribution** written on the side.
What does this imply about the other people who run similar businesses?

While traveling, you will need to stop in to rest stops and do your duty. I saw the handwritten message, **Homward Bound** in one of the stalls.
Obviously, this person is not returning from university studies. If so, he certainly isn't majoring in English – at least I hope not. Didn't those two words represent the name of a song from a few years ago by Sighmin & Gharfunkall?

I saw the sign for an ***antique mall***.
I haven't done much research, but I didn't think those shopping venues were that old.

On a trip to Canada and Minnesota in June of 2006, somewhere on the way to Thunder Bay, I passed signs for ***18 mile creek*** and ***6 mile lake***.
Since I was driving in Canada, shouldn't the signs have said, 28.8 kilometer creek and 9.6 kilometer lake?

I entered a restaurant in western Ohio to get some breakfast. The waitress said I could sit anywhere. I sat down in the lap of this beautiful woman. She wasn't very happy so I moved to a table that was empty. I shouldn't have listened to this server.

While on interstate 94 in Wisconsin, I noticed the exit signs didn't mark the roads with numbers, but with letters, such as ***Q*** and ***PP***.
Apparently someone ran off with the numbers and you can't gamble in the state. Maybe the runners took them all, so you can make bets after all, only smaller. Just make sure you can cover your losses.

On the interstate in Illinois, I saw the sign, ***Illinois 47*** along the highway. Since I was in the state, this couldn't indicate how many miles to go before I reached it.
Maybe it was a partial score.

In July 2006, I was forced to take a scary anti-inflammatory so I read the side of the container for this drug. It said, *Take 1 tablet twice daily by mouth.*
I figured putting it in my ear wouldn't be effective. Thank God, I don't have to get it into my body by putting it some place else, enema style.

A truck passed me and on the back were displayed the words, ***All natural cheese.***
I don't eat much cheese but I can't see how anyone else would even try the alternative, unnatural cheese.

I got an invitation to a fiftieth wedding anniversary party with the words, ***No silver please.***
I guess I can't bring the Lone Ranger's horse as a gift.

I had a checking account with a certain bank, but I closed it, as I wasn't happy with their service. They changed their name to ***Citizens Bank***, with the understanding that the customer would be served better by that alteration. Let me assure you, modifying a name of a company won't help consumers in the least – it takes real effort. I thought about taking a gun to that bank and getting some cash. After all, if it was a bank for us citizens, couldn't I have some money from them?
I didn't do that – I didn't feel like spending time in the can with former Congressmen.

On a trip home from a vacation in Maine during September 2006, I noticed a sign for ***Bates College***. That must be the school to go to after graduating from Bates High School.
Carrie on!

I close the chapter with a few words that you can find on signs and bumper stickers.

Don't blame us – we voted for the other guy

One nation under surveillance

Another patriot for peace

99

Draft Richard Perle

Mainstream white guys for peace

Think – it's not illegal yet

Let's bomb Texas – they have oil too

How did our oil get under their sand?

If you can't pronounce it, don't bomb it

Don't cheat – the government hates competition

Happiness is seeing a lawyer's picture on a milk carton

I changed this last one slightly.

10. Happy hour

If you read my cookbook, you may recall a visit from my friend Spike to my home in New Jersey in the late 1960s. I lived in Clifton, New Jersey on a street called Sheridan Avenue, if I remember correctly. However, in the words of Paul Harvey, here's the rest of the story.

After dinner one evening on that visit, we decided to head over to the Big Apple. Both of us were into fruit. As far as I can recall – it was a long time ago, so give me some slack – I drove my Chevy II and we landed up in the Village. Spike seemed to be in charge of getting us to our destination and we wound up at 15 East 7th Street, the home of the world famous McSorley's Bar. The ale was good and we probably should have stopped buying drafts a great deal sooner than we did. We were feeling no pain and eventually we got home, early in the morning.

Unfortunately, it wasn't early enough and the morning came too quickly. It was a school day and I was supposed to be teaching but somehow I thought better of facing my students. I called in and reported sick – it really wasn't a lie. I went back to bed and recovered. A few hours later, Spike made a suggestion for what to do that day. We headed over to Shea Stadium to see the Mets play some baseball. When you're young, you can recover from sickness quite quickly. The home team lost in a pitchers' battle 12-9, but that season they did win the World Series.

When I think back to those two days, I wonder what I would have said if my principal or vice principal had been at the game. Even teachers have temporary brain deficiencies, especially the younger ones. As delightful as it is, McSorley's ale doesn't help to keep people on the straight and narrow.

Seventeen years later I was older and wiser. On this occasion I brought my friend Bill down to the Village in

New York City in the spring of 1986. I figured he would like McSorley's Bar, so off we went. If you are ever down in that area, check it out – it has a great deal of history. If you can't find it, ask and people should direct you to it. If they can't help you find it, ask a policeman or fireman. If they don't know where it is, no one does.

On this trip, we were getting close to the tavern and the closer we got, the louder was the singing. The strains – definitely an appropriate word – were emanating from the bar. The song that was attempted to be sung seemed to be our glorious National Anthem, sung at the top of the lungs of the crowd. Somehow I felt we were almost at McSorley's. When it was finished, you may have expected to hear the cry, "Play ball," but that wasn't what followed. Instead we heard, "Boston sucks." On that day, the Yankees weren't playing their hated foes, the Red Sox.

"Happy Hour" does strange things to people. You could say that the amount of intelligence decreases as more drink is imbibed. It is a scientific fact that beer chugging and throwing down the shots does indeed destroy brain cells so it's probably not far from the truth. At the same time, over the years a great deal of humor has evolved from this national obsession. Here are a few bar stories for your pleasure. Most, if not all, are fabrications.

A jumper cable walks into a bar. The bartender says, "I'll serve you, but don't start anything."
He probably would have been more welcome at the American Graffiti Bar.

This duck walks into a bar and orders a beer. "Four bucks," says the bartender.
"Put it on my bill," the duck replied.
*He finished the drink and got **down** off the stool.*

A dyslexic man walks into a rab.
I wonder if he ordered an ela elap.

A man walks into a bar with a slab of asphalt under his arm and says, "A beer please, and one for the road."
*The jukebox was playing **Highway to Hell**.*

A dog with his leg wrapped in bandages hobbles into a saloon. He sidles up to the bar and announces: "I'm lookin' fer the man who shot my paw."
Did he look in the pawpaw patch?

A neutron walks into a bar. "I'd like a beer," he says. The bartender promptly serves up a beer. "How much will that be?" asks the neutron.
"For you?" replies the bartender, "no charge."
If you don't get that one, you probably cut physics class.

A skeleton walks into a bar and says, "Gimme a beer, and a mop."
He wouldn't have needed the mop if he ordered some dry wine.

A termite walks into a bar and says, "Is the bar tender here?"
The bartender replied, "I think you'd be happier at the Mahogany Room on Pine Street or the Cedar Bar on Maple."

A man walks into a bar with an alligator. He asks the bartender if he serves politicians. The bartender says he does, so the man says, "I'll have a Guinness and Croc will have a Senator."
They finished, left the bar and the guy says to the reptile, "Your posture's bad. You're leaning to the right."

103

Four fonts walk into a bar. The barman says "Oi - get out! We don't want your type in here."
The Fonz was having a pale ale not far away when one of the fonts says, "Why is he allowed in here?"

Two peanuts walk into a bar. One was a salted.
They left the other nut home. He was saying, "Cashew" too much.

This next one came from the buffet at halftime.

Two cannibals are eating a clown. One says to the other, "Does this taste funny to you?"
Yeah, I think it needs more Tabasco sauce. Perhaps, it's Cathy's Clown.

People do some weird things and others may blame it on the moon. It's difficult to rationalize that connection when these things happen in the middle of the day. We shouldn't blame this stuff on *Happy Hour*, either. There has to be another explanation.

June 25, 2005 was one of those days for me. It started on the Ellicott Creek Trailway, where I daily walk about three or four miles. On that Saturday morning, I spotted a couple hauling a small wagon, the kind we played with as kids. It wasn't an unusual sight except that they had two five-gallon water jugs on it. It was a hot day so these people weren't taking any chances about getting dehydrated.
It turns out they were just watering the flowers. They wouldn't have had a hose long enough to reach from their home.
Two hours later I headed out to the library and checked out three books. The librarian commented that she liked my t-shirt. It was the red ethnic one with the Polish eagle on it and the word, "Nazdrowie." The lady then asked

me what it meant and I pronounced the word and explained that it is a toast, meaning, "Here's to you." Maybe she just liked the color red because I doubt if her name ended in "ski."

I proceeded from the library to a card shop to pick up a birthday card as well as a fiftieth wedding anniversary card. I gave the clerk a ten dollar bill and a dime, hoping to get back quarters instead of dimes and nickels in change. You can never have too many quarters if you have to feed the laundromat. She asked if I should take the amount out of what I have handed to her. I replied yes but missed a great opportunity. I should have said, "No, take it from the money of the customer next to me."

Didn't these clerks take geometry?

I left to fill up my car with gasoline. While driving on the auxiliary road to the pumps, I noticed a woman driving parallel to me, heading in the same direction. However, she was driving through lined spaces of the parking lot. Fortunately these spaces were all empty.

I'm not sure the same didn't apply to her brain.

This next offering is almost unbelievable, but I'll relate it anyway.

In September 2005 at Northern Ireland's Belfast Zoo, Phoebe (her real name) the chimp and two of her friends snuck out of their compound and had to be rounded up. Armed security guards fired shots into the air to frighten the animals and not only did Phoebe's entourage become more docile, they put their hands up.

These animals are probably watching too many episodes of COPS.

In July 2005, London's *Sunday Telegraph* reported that due to the shortage of supplies for the military stationed in Iraq and Afghanistan, soldiers of the British Army were

requested to shout, "bang, bang" in place of firing practice rounds.
Our government should try that. There would be fewer casualties and you could save a great deal of money on bullets.

A certain very "intelligent" engineer worked with a friend of mine's husband at Calspan, formerly Cornell Lab. He once came to work with his hair all messed up. It seems he and his wife just moved and he couldn't find a comb. The same guy came in one day wearing his wife's boots. He said he couldn't find his own.
Maybe he just wanted to look like Einstein. It might have been quite embarrassing if he couldn't have found his socks and underwear.

11. You blinked and missed it

If you don't open your eyes, you'll miss out on so much. A great deal of what you observe is very funny.

General George Custer was involved with the wrong kind of "stand." He would have lived longer if his name had been "Custard!"

It's taken a while but I think I have discovered Victoria's Secret.

I am thinking about getting indirect TV.
Someone told me that late at night you head over to your neighbor's house when he's asleep, cut into his cable setup, add a signal splitter and hook up your television. Make sure you get enough coaxial cable.

They say that those who can't teach become guidance counselors. I recall a few that were competent but there was one of which I wasn't so sure. During my last year of teaching at John Jay High School in Hopewell Junction, New York, a counselor sent me a student who didn't speak English. Pedrough LaRoo – not his real name and not misspelled, just ask his parents – was a bright lad even though he was deaf and wasn't familiar with the language I used to teach mathematics. However, the note that came with him mentioned that he could lip read his native tongue. I was quite relieved since all my classes come with subtitles in French.
The only thing made-up here is the name.

On October 15th I got a case of spring fever.

On June 24, 2005 I received a letter dated June 30, 2005 from a car dealership. Who said time machines don't exist. This reminds me of a morning a few years back. At the time I was still consulting and was forced to rise from my bed at all kinds of ungodly hours. In the car on my way to work, I had on the *Art Bell* program. Those of you not familiar with his agenda, it's a great show if you have an open mind and don't rule out conspiracies.

A young man called in and mentioned that he recently was released from jail and would resume his project. That involved building a time machine. Apparently that is what got him into trouble. In order to get his contraption working, he needed a transformer. He saw a used one in the field and figured no one would miss it so it soon had a new owner. He then proceeded to build his machine. If you lived near him, you had a pretty good idea when he was operating. Invariably, your lights would dim and maybe even a few circuit breakers in your house would have to be reset. If you are still one of his neighbors, you may want to consider moving.

While we are discussing the paranormal, I finished reading a book on the Loch Ness monster. I was talking to a friend of mine about the book and somehow we strayed to the topic of UFOs. He then asked why there hadn't been any reported sightings recently, specifically since the end of the 1980s. Apparently when the aliens looked at who was in the White House, they figured that there was no intelligent life on the planet and left.

I live outside Buffalo close to the University at Buffalo North Campus. I mentioned the Ellicott Creek Trailway earlier. I try to use it every day. While on the paths, I see roller bladers, joggers and bicyclists in addition to those just out for a stroll. On occasion I have even seen joggers pushing strollers and even bike riders with a baby following behind in a carriage. Recently I saw a child on roller blades. He was being followed by his mom, who also had on a pair of blades as she held on to the family dog. I thought of asking why the canine didn't have roller blades. I didn't, though. A few days later I witnessed a pair jogging with one of them holding on to a leash that held a retriever. I wonder what would have happened if the lab decided he just wanted to walk and stopped jogging.

As I was checking out of the supermarket in March 2006, the clerk started putting my groceries into the cart, except it wasn't the cart I used while shopping. The person who had just checked out wanted to use it and said the cart was hers. The cashier took care of this, putting my stuff into the cart close to me. I didn't show off my intelligence but rather kept my mouth shut – I wanted to tell the shopper ahead of me that all the carts belong to the supermarket.

Police are considering using the *Mini Cooper* to chase down speeders. They plan to put a jet engine in the back and change the name to the *Mini Copper*.

In Chatham, New Brunswick, the Rotary Club said that the grand prize in its raffle to emphasize environmental awareness will be a Hummer.
*For those of you who haven't heard, **Hummer** rhymes with* dumber.

I'm really confused by some of the terms applied to the way we dress. Of course there's "black tie" and "formal" as well as "business" dress and "casual." However, the world of business in their infinite wisdom came up with "business casual," whatever that means. This was to accommodate the relaxation of the dress code on Fridays. Perhaps they would have been better off to say "no ties and sport coat" or "no suits." Personally, I don't think anyone really knows what this phrase means.

Some years ago I interviewed for a software contract in Western New York wearing a suit. I was awarded the position and told to report the following Monday with the stipulation that attire was – you guessed it – "business casual." On the day I reported for work wearing the obvious shoes, socks, underwear, etc. as well as a dress shirt and jeans, I was told that the latter weren't allowed. However, there were individuals at the office wearing "painter's pants," even though they were only working with a computer and not a paintbrush. I was allowed to stay that day and work in the attire I just described.

I believe pants – with paint on them – are acceptable.

Not long ago Cathy Guisewite in her Sunday comic "Cathy" got into this same topic. It was a gas and I even clipped it and posted it to my refrigerator for a time. She mentioned an invitation to a Halloween Party where the attire was "costume casual." If the phrase had been "business costume casual," would that mean you could dress up as a gorilla but would need to wear a suit? Could you come dressed as a salesman? I'm thrilled to have left that rat race and now that I think of it, should have retired sooner.

One day I was in Borders and saw a guy reading. Nonetheless, it looked as though he was asleep. He didn't fall off the chair, at least while I was in the store. Maybe he was glued to the seat.

From some of the people I have met who work at book stores, I figured he was an employee.

I was out one day and saw an "Outback" trailer on Maple Avenue, not far from where I live. But it was parked in the front and not out back.

Twice a year, we have to adjust our clocks for daylight savings time. It was the fall of the year and someone mentioned to me that there is a two-hour time difference between the east and west coasts. I always thought it was three but maybe that changed. After doing some checking I verified that indeed there was a difference of three hours. *Whoever told me this is probably watching too many episodes of* **The Twilight Zone**

I once sang in a chorus and someone mentioned that one song would be done, *a capella*, that is, without music.

She was so dumb, she thought she could use Pearl Jam on her toast.

He was so dumb, he thought M&M peanut was a rap CD.

While making out, when his girlfriend said lower, he deepened his voice.

Show me where Stalin's buried and I'll show you a communist plot.

When she told me I was average, she was just being mean.

I went with a friend of mine to a sporting goods store because he wanted to buy some camouflage trousers. I wandered over to the camping section. When I got done, I looked for him but I couldn't find him.

There were two ships. One was red and the other one blue. They collided. At last report, the survivors were marooned.

The easiest way to solve the problem of something lost around the house is to buy a replacement.

I was on an elevator the other day, and the operator kept calling me "son." I said, "Why do you call me 'son?' You're not my father."

He said, "I brought you up, didn't I?"

Yesterday I began the North Beach diet. You can eat anything you want but they make no promises. I'm told it's as good as the South Beach diet. That's assuring.

A friend of mine just got back from a trip to Budapest. I asked him what he thought of the Buddha.

Recently I saw a book at the supermarket on "Internet Poker for Dummies." There are all kinds of these books, such as "Computers for Dummies," and the list goes on. I guess I'm fortunate because of this, for without it, this book wouldn't be possible.

Steven Wright said that you can't have everything. Where would you put it? If you had everything, you'd have a place for it. My friend said that his mother-in-law wouldn't have a problem, either. She'd just put it up in the attic. Nonetheless, you'd have a great deal of clutter and I hope you don't mind yard sales.

Some time ago I needed some material so I contacted an agency to get directions to where they were located. I told them where I was, but unfortunately they couldn't tell me how to get there. I was trying to get a Triptik from the American Automobile Association.

In May of 2005, I received a postcard from a dental arts firm, which said, "Enter to win a colored TV." I doubt that this is the appliance that people of color have in their homes. Maybe it's just the result of the kids playing with cans of spray paint.

One night my dreams were in black and white.
I need to talk to Ted Turner.

Many times a host at a party will ask you if you care for pretzels or chips. I recently saw a bag of snack food that eliminates your need to make a decision in this regard. It's called "pretzel chips." I have no idea what they are and why anyone would want to buy them.

I was looking for some prunes recently at the supermarket but from the looks of the shelves, they've run out.

I've got good news for George, Donald, Dick and Condi – I found the yellow cake. It's one of the choices along with banana pudding, pumpkin pie, cherry pie, chocolate mint and vanilla ice cream at one of the four big mess halls at the U. S. base at Balad. This information comes from page 417 of *Fiasco: The American Military Adventure in Iraq* by Thomas E. Ricks.
Its only purpose is dessert, although I'm sure it could be used in a food fight.

My niece Elizabeth went to Italy in May 2006 to study art and enjoy a short respite from the everyday grind of work after obtaining her degree from the University at Buffalo. She sent me an email about her first few days in Rome, observing that "traffic lights there are just suggestions."
That's about the same as the driving behavior here in the United States.

On June 29, 2006, I noticed that my calendar in the kitchen had a June 31st.
Why didn't someone tell me about this? By the way, this is a calendar from the university.

113

Someone called me the square root of 5. They must think I'm a radical.

If you don't get that one, you didn't take enough math classes. I put this in for my high school geometry teacher to get a laugh.

My arthritis is acting up so much it should be nominated for an Academy award.

I don't get my news from the Fox network or CNN, especially about politics. Instead, I listen to what's happening on NPR, but not religiously.

I believe in separation of church and state.

I would never name my kid, *Chuckie*. People would either think his last name is *Cheese* or that he is an evil puppet.

There are a lot of crazies out there. I headed out the door to do some grocery shopping, and going to my car I passed another one parked, from which I heard conversation. The car was not running, but there was someone behind the wheel talking on a cell phone. It was a real scorcher outside, with the temperature close to 90 degrees. All intelligence in this case was not evaporated, as the windows of the vehicle were open.

I parked my Subaru and approached the supermarket. On the way in, I spied a gentleman carrying groceries looking perplexed. It appeared that he couldn't find his car. I thought about mentioning to him that I saw a car being towed by the shopping police, but instead I entered the store.

In the first chapter of ***for seeing eye dogs only***, I mentioned a government study to see why people hated beets. You'll be happy to know that you, the taxpayer paid for this one hundred thousand dollar venture. As part of a

114

food co-operative that I joined in 2006, one week the bag of groceries had beets, but they were yellow, rather than the normal color one expects. I think I may have discovered how we can get people to eat beets and actually like them. It won't cost a cent, either. The secret is to use the beets similar to the ones I recently ate and not tell the person at the dinner table what they were eating. If the majority of people likes them, it means that the problem has to do with the color or the name itself. Since we took care of the color concept – I like the color purple – we can simply give the vegetable a new name, something French. How about, *le beet goson?*

I got a telephone call and was told that in the future I should never leave a message on that individual's answering machine. Those things are unreliable. I should always be sure to talk to this caller directly, not through a telephone-recording device. This person went on, emphasizing this point.
I did not actually hear this person in the flesh. This admonition was a message – maybe sermon is a better word here – on my answering machine.

I was thinking of going back to school so I applied to the Electoral College.
I understand there's a wide selection of electives.

I get some emails for people who are inventors. I have one idea that I can't reveal because then you might steal it and start marketing. I have another idea, which I discovered by accident: a non-toxic glue. Isn't that the way with much of innovation?
In November 2006, the **Sunday Magazine** of the **Buffalo News** had a recipe for chicken and vegetable tangine. It consists of eggplant, chicken, onions, tomatoes, almonds and a few spices that make up a very nice curry. I didn't have the first ingredient so I tried the dish without it

115

and it was very good. On two occasions when I ate the dish over rice, I used a steak knife for the meat and when I was finished, I left it on the plate and didn't do the dishes right away. The next day, there was a strong bond between the cutting utensil and the plate – I came up with a new glue. I doubt that I will market it, so you're welcome to do with it what you wish.

Father Nicholas Swiatek is an O.F.M. Conventual Franciscan. As you may have surmised, he is also my brother. In the summer of 2006, he was in the hospital for a colon resection and while I visited him during his recovery, he told the nurse that his level of pain was a 3. Most hospitals have a chart on the wall with the ten different levels, based from 1 to 10 – 1 being no pain. This system needs to be revamped since it's difficult to make a judgment if you haven't been instructed in the various distinctions. I propose the following:

I feel good (James Brown style) – no pain
Some pain
A lot of pain (that's hospital jargon)
Give me a shot of Demerol – a great deal of pain
Load the gun – it doesn't get any worse

I heard the words of another Christmas Song – you're all familiar with the words. I'll have to tell my mom that in a few years, the wishes won't be for her. You know the phrase I'm talking about, "And so I'm offering this simple phrase, for kids from one to ninety two."
Newborns get left out, too.

If you take the word, "bullish," shift over one letter and add another, you get another word. Take either of these two words and drop a few letters and you get the name of a president.

116

From the comments before and some that will follow, you might feel that "working for the government" is an oxymoron. That might be true but let me assure you that they have no monopoly on incompetence and laziness – corporate America qualifies in this regard as well. I have heard of so many examples of people employed in the business world who do as little as possible.

I asked a friend if he was thinking of retiring. He mentioned that he might do so if he got the right package. Then he said that he doesn't do anything at his present job. I asked him, "If you are doing nothing, how do you know when you're finished?"

12. We report – you decide

I have chosen not to watch Fox News, or CNN for that matter, even though the latter gets my vote over the former. As far as ABC, CBS and NBC, they are no better an alternative and it would be more appropriate to use the word, *news entertainment* to describe their coverage. Even PBS is starting to trouble me as a source of information as they are too much concerned with balance, which should only apply to trapeze artists and budgets – that second idea may be as obsolete as wise men in the executive branch of government. With people like Jason Blair and Judith Miller, even papers like the *New York Slimes, Wall Street Urinal* and *Washington Boast* have lost a great deal of respect, especially with their irresponsibility over the years.

The evening news has morphed into the evening blues. Now more than ever, we need relief from all the pestilence, corruption, crime, war and violence. The following offerings are an attempt to see the humor in the headline and stories. I have added a few comments in italics following the headlines.

I read this headline on the Yahoo home page on January 10, 2007:
Yale a cappella group beaten up while on tour
Maybe they should have rehearsed more!

I saw this headline on December 16, 2006:
Researchers cure diabetes in mice 'overnight'
If you didn't feed them all those Crunch bars, you wouldn't have those rodent problems.

The news in the first week of December 2006 mentioned that the United States wasn't winning the war in Iraq, but they weren't losing it, either.
Apparently, we must be in overtime.

A headline on the Internet on November 29, 2006 stated:

More employees call in 'sick' during holidays

I hope they didn't spend money on a study to reach this conclusion. Calling in sick is probably from stuffing their face too much.

There's been a lot of controversy between East and West during 2006 and this headline on October 25, 2006 was no exception:

China says N. Korea not planning test

*I thought the Bush administration was really into this testing thing, as illustrated by his **No Child's Behind Left** agenda. Thanks go out to Greg Palast for **Armed Madhouse**.*

On October 24, 2006, I saw this headline just before logging on to check my email:

Ethiopia's 3.2 million-year-old 'Lucy' to tour U.S.

I know she is no longer with us, but I didn't think the actress was that old – her show was on in the last century!

Before getting my email on Saturday, August 26, 2006, Yahoo had this headline:

China cracks down on striptease funerals

Costs for dressing the body are a great deal less.

The following headline appeared on the Web on August 24, 2006:

Astronomers declare Pluto no longer a planet

Won't Walt and Mickey be upset?

The following headline appeared on the Web on August 15, 2006:

Seven dwarfs more well-known than U.S. judges

Is that a bad thing?

120

The following headline appeared on the Web on July 26, 2006:

More Americans too heavy for X-rays, scans
Are they doing those procedures with scales, now?

The following headline appeared on the Web on June 2, 2006:

Rice warns Iran it doesn't have much time
She should tell them about daylight savings time.

On June 1, 2006, I saw the following headline on the Internet:

Cordless Jump-Rope Can Help the Clumsy
*Will the user be able to see it? Are they going to market it as **virtual rope**?*

On May 18, 2006, I heard a news story that mentioned more money would be spent on shoe bomb detection equipment.
Couldn't this cost be avoided by prohibiting shoes on board planes? The airline could sell flip-flops and this would help create a few jobs. Am I mistaken, but doesn't bomb detection equipment find explosives no matter where they are positioned?

On July 14, 2006, I was tuned into NPR radio and I heard something about President Bush being in St. Petersburg, Russia to meet the Russian leader.
Unfortunately, Putin was in St. Petersburg, Florida, so it doesn't look like they will be in each other's presence that weekend. At least the two guys are traveling and seeing the world.

On the weekend of June 25, 2005, a young girl was attacked and killed by a shark. Not long after that a young boy was attacked and survived but needed to have his leg

121

amputated. Both events took place off the Florida coast. On June 28, I heard a report on National Public Radio about these incidents. The reporter said, "Experts don't think these attacks are related."

How do they know this? Did these "experts" interview the family or the neighbors of the attackers?

"He never bothered us and was very quiet. He seemed like such a nice shark."

U.S., Iraqi troops continue their sweep

The above headline made news on St. Patrick's Day in 2006.

So, are they going into the housecleaning business? Maybe they should contact the Swiffer Boat Veterans for Truth – see Chapter 15.

Ohio Man to Social Security: I'm Not Dead

The above headline was in the news on Saturday, March 4, 2006. He's talking, so he must be alive. Send him his social security check.

I wonder if this guy is related to someone in Greenville County, South Carolina. It's not quite the same but you may have read about another individual who is deceased. This didn't stop the government from trying to contact him – and that was without a medium or ouija board. Perhaps, the authorities just confused the two individuals. If you still aren't familiar with what I'm talking about, you'll have to read the last chapter of **The Read My Lips Cookbook** *to understand the connection.*

Democrats want immediate vote on port deal

This is another headline from the same day.

Why not leave that up to the oenologists? Don't the politicians have enough to deal with?

The Buffalo News / Sunday, November 6, 2005
Luxury cruise ship outruns pirates off Somalia
I thought "be a pirate day" was in October.

This headline appeared in the news on Friday March 10, 2006:
Talabani Convenes Parliament for March 19
Do you think that perhaps this guy should change his name?

Bush orders staff to attend briefings on ethics, secrets
Wouldn't the same effect be accomplished with booster shots?

30,000 layoffs coming at GM
I didn't think there were that many jobs left there.

The United States recalls its ambassador to Syria
Why? Was she defective?

Top Shiite welcomes Sunni overtures
I didn't even know they had an orchestra!

The following information was released as stories in the news. What follows is the gist of each.

One of the stories in the news of Friday March 10, 2006 was dissatisfaction with the current administration. The article mentioned, "More and more people, particularly Republicans, disapprove of President Bush's performance." *Maybe that's why he didn't get an Oscar nomination.*

More information was released about the budget for intelligence affairs.
I thought those liaisons were gone when Clinton left office.

President George W. Bush refused to comment on the situation in Syria, saying he needed more intelligence.
He said it, not me.

On June 6, 2005, there was a new ruling on marijuana use.
Does that mean that there won't be any joint press conferences?

Here is one story you will never see in the news.

Sources say that the link between **Iraq** and **Al Qaeda** has been proven. Both are examples of words where a Q is not followed by a **u**.
Vanna may be able to help here.

Thanks to Joe Bernardi of Martinsburg, West Virginia for the following headline:
According to the Washington Post of March 20, 2005, one of the games in today's Women's NCAA tournament is the Duke Blue Devils vs. the Canisius College Golden Griffiths.
Hmmm, is a griffith a female griffin, or are we talking here about the birth of a nation?

What follow are reputed to be actual headlines and supposedly the best ones for the year 2005.

New Study of Obesity Looks for Larger Test Group
They probably won't be able to enter through the double doors.

Crack Found on Governor's Daughter
That sounds like a skin problem – all she needs is a good moisturizer.

Is There a Ring of Debris around Uranus?
Isn't that question too personal? The press has no shame.

Something went wrong in Jet crash, expert says
Maybe this guy could figure out who killed JFK.

Police Begin Campaign to Run Down Jaywalkers
Won't they get blood on the cars?

Panda Mating Fails: Veterinarian Takes Over
Didn't that upset the spouse?

Miners Refuse to Work after Death
Don't worry – they can get a job with the government.

Juvenile Court to Try Shooting Defendant
That should cut down court costs.

War Dims Hope for Peace
Halliburton's not complaining.

Cold Wave Linked to Temperatures
Is that Celsius or Fahrenheit?

Kids make Nutritious Snacks
I wouldn't know – I'm a vegetarian. I wonder if they taste like chicken?

Hospitals are Sued by Seven Foot Doctors
Those guys should be playing basketball – there's more money in that profession.

Typhoon Rips Through Cemetery; 100s Dead
It would have been worse if the typhoon hit a store on Boxing Day.

Astronaut Takes Blame for Gas in Spacecraft
The departure meal next time probably won't be enchiladas and refried beans.

London Couple Slain; Police Suspect Homicide
Were these investigators originally from Los Angeles?

Red Tape Holds Up New Bridges!
Duct tape would have worked at half the cost.

Man Struck By Lightning: Faces Battery Charge
He wouldn't have if he had gotten ohm sooner.

Local High School Dropouts Cut In Half
At least biology class will have specimens.

13. Crime still doesn't pay

It appears that those who insist on a life of crime haven't read my 2005 book. I should send some copies to the prisons. Besides a few laughs, it gave some advice about the trade. The chapter on criminal behavior should have been helpful. The incompetence of these novices continues along with the hysterics.

Some people will steal anything. A few years ago I was out riding my 10-speed when suddenly I experienced a flat tire. I should not have been surprised since both tires were bald. The bike was a few years old and ready to be replaced. Nonetheless, I placed it in the ditch along the side of the road so no one would spot it and started to walk home to pick up my car. Upon my arrival to fetch the bike, there was no sign of it.

If that last theft wasn't stupid enough, even more recently, thieves broke into my home while I was away on a very short vacation and ripped off some electronic equipment. They didn't take any cash since there wasn't any in the house but they left with a word processor – which I missed – a tape cassette deck and video cassette recorder. I only wish they had not left my television and stereo receiver, since I wanted to replace them anyway. The two recorders they got were on their last legs.

Needah Mafix was arrested in Cincinnati in June 2005 and pleaded guilty to possession of cocaine but refused to provide a DNA sample to the authorities. The reason he gave was that he feared being cloned. However, the prosecutor mentioned that he didn't think the state wanted another Mafix.
When the aliens came to his hometown, they saw him and left.

In Fostoria, Ohio, thieves broke into a building that serves the poor in late winter of 2005. They stole a safe from the Fostoria Bureau of Concern but what they confiscated turned out to be empty. Moreover, director Susan Simpkins added that it was a piece of junk and she had been searching for some one to remove it from the premises.

Not only are they dumb, at times they can be helpful.

Ivan Dumbfounded was arrested when he reported to the 90th Precinct station house in Brooklyn to check on the status of his friend, Kaut N. Theact. He probably wouldn't have been apprehended except that he stood in front of his own "wanted" poster, the one that had him alongside Kaut.

He apparently never heard of the nose and glasses disguise.

A few guys decided to make counterfeit quarters, but the neighbors complained to the police about the noise made by the stamping machines. So the guys got caught. But an analysis of the counterfeit quarters showed that they each contained 27 cents worth of silver.

Right now they're probably making silver license plates.

Likum Young was being questioned by Federal agents relative to child pornography charges when a screen saver featuring child-sex images showed up on his PC. He pleaded guilty in June 2005.

Police captured Leva Mealone in Clovis, NH after they followed a trail of blood coming from the perpetrator's body due to a glass encounter at the scene of the crime. Actually the authorities concluded later that the blood came about when Leva accidentally smashed his head with a hammer while robbing a church. As if that wasn't bad enough, the bag with the jewelry broke and he lost most of what he had stolen.

He didn't say enough prayers in church before robbing it.

In Peterborough, England in July 2005, criminals made off with a two-foot high statue of St. Anthony of Padua. The latter is the patron saint of lost and stolen items. *I don't believe there is a patron saint of dumbbells.*

You probably shouldn't call the police and report that someone stole your illegal drugs, but that's exactly what Ivan Dumbashell of Bellevue, Illinois did in September of 2005. It doesn't end there as he mentioned to the officer that his neighbor swiped his marijuana plants. Going to the place where they should have been, he and the police official saw that the cannabis was still there. He was charged with growing weed and admitted that he might have had a bit to drink when all this happened.
Maybe Ivan should be a legislator.

Along the same line, Donna B. Scared and Gladys Goodstuff were arrested for their cash crop in Clarkston, Washington. Police were chasing a bear through the neighborhood and the commotion led the hashish harvesters to throw their plant out the window over a high fence, fearing a drug bust. It landed in the wrong place and you could say that the result was a potted policeman.
I always felt being a farmer was too challenging a way to make a living.

Another organization that has to be classified as crooked is the IRS. Maybe they don't really meet this classification and they're only missing intelligence. I'm convinced it's at least one of those two. An earlier chapter pointed out what those letters really stand for. I wouldn't complain if they did their job. Unfortunately, from my dealing with these incompetents, I can only conclude that in order to fulfill a task, you have to know what it is. Maybe that's why they're so annoying to everyday citizens.

Not that long ago, I was audited by these nincompoops. I decided to cooperate and maybe that was the mistake I made. I was ready to provide what they wanted but thought that I should get as much information from them as I could just to make sure that I was right and they weren't. I obtained their own guidelines, read them and found that indeed I had filed my taxes in the proper manner and the case should be closed. I provided matching documentation to them, but in the end, they nonetheless claimed I owed them money. I probably should have insisted that they were wrong, but I already had a lawyer and he felt it was in my best interest to go along with their erroneous ways.

If you think this is unusual, have you ever called their office for tax advice, used their advice to file your taxes and then were later told that what you did was not according to the guidelines for filling out a return? I rest my case.

14. Fun things to do

Too often young children say they are bored. I find that hard to believe with all the books, video games and nuclear reactor kits that these kids have at their disposal. Grownups may not say it but they have the same problem at times, although these very people also insist that they don't have enough time. Here are a few ideas to add excitement and cause others to shake their heads. The author is not responsible for any injuries or lawsuits, and will not provide bond for any reader who tries these suggestions.

I haven't tried this but instead of the usual dull message on your answering machine, why not place a "busy signal?" This should thwart the telemarketers but you'll have to tell your friends that they can leave a message after the busy tone.

You can eliminate most telemarketers by getting involved with the "Do not call" movement and for me it seemed to eliminate many of those pests. However, there are others who will still keeping ringing your phone at all hours, such as charities and companies that you deal with – banks and credit card companies. What you can do to drive these clowns crazy and have some fun at the same time is to say, "Hold on, please." You'll know when you can return to the phone to hang it up because you will hear, "If you'd like to make a call, please hang up and dial again."

If your phone has caller ID, check the incoming number before you answer the phone and use that knowledge to greet the caller with his or her name. When they ask how you knew it was them, say, "Somehow I had a premonition it was you."

If you don't have caller ID, answer the phone by saying, "Hello, Chris," or "Hello, Pat." If you happen to guess right, use the same response as if you actually had caller ID. Otherwise, when the caller says it's Tom or Judy, say, "Sorry, I must have the wrong number and hang up."

You can have a great deal of fun with the telephone – one of the worse inventions of all time. I'm not married but some time ago, I received a phone call. The person on the other end asked for my wife. I told her she wasn't home, and that really wasn't a lie. This person should have then asked if I was hitched but instead inquired when my spouse would be there. I responded that I couldn't say. Again, I didn't lie – I wasn't sure when I was going to get married.

Another great thing to do after the phone rings is pretend that you're a thief who just broke in to the house. If they ask for a specific person, just say that may have been the individual you had to shoot – he wouldn't shut up. You'd be surprised how fast telemarketers hang up the phone.

It doesn't happen very often but you might receive a call from a dating service. There's a surefire way to get the party calling to hang up the phone. Complain that the last date they set you up with so expensive, you had to go over your credit card limit to buy concrete for your date's shoes. Of course, it was worth it.

You pay for your phone service, so why not take advantage of it? Say you had a really bad mathematics teacher in college. Call him and disguise your voice so it sounds like one of his colleagues. You may want to imitate one with whose voice he isn't that familiar, like a new guy in the department. Tell him you just solved Fermat's Last Theorem and stress the fact that it was really easy, just as

132

Fermat claimed. For extra authenticity, call at two or three in the morning. You may want to call from a pay phone.

Many times you will be waiting for an elevator and someone will approach the area and press the up button, which is lit up since you already touched that same button earlier. Ask him if he's read my book, *for seeing eye dogs only*. Tell him it's about missing intelligence.

How many times have people come up to you, pointed to their wrist and then asked for the time? If you know it, tell him what time it is and then point to an area of your body just below the stomach and ask them where the bathroom is?

You can do this at a department store like K-Mart. Don't do it at Wal-Mart, as you should really boycott their store until they change their labor practices. Go into one of the fitting rooms and yell loud enough for management of the store to hear, "Hey! We're out of toilet paper in here!" On second thought, try it at *Lord & Taylor*.

You may not want to do the next suggestion on this same visit, but save it for your next trip to this department store – as long as you're not banned. Walk up to an employee and tell her in an official tone, "Code 3 in housewares," and see what happens. If you were allowed in the store this time, you probably will at least be forever forbidden or hauled off to an awful destiny. You might want to wear a disguise.
Don't ask me what a "code 3" is – I never tried this. I may suggest these things, but I'm not that dumb.

You can do this at any store that sells time devices. Set all the alarm clocks in housewares to go off at five minute intervals. Be careful that you don't get caught doing this – prison life is something you may want to avoid.

You can have some fun in sporting goods stores. Here's a way to do that. Set up a tent in the camping department and tell other shoppers you'll only invite them in if they bring pillows from the bedding department. You may need to stop in the section for ammunition first.

If you did go to the hunting department, you should pick up a gun and then ask the clerk if he knows where the anti-depressants are. You could also take some liquid from your water bottle, apply it to your forehead, pick up a large hunting knife and ask the clerk if they have any machetes? *You probably won't make it to the area where they sell tents.*

Every store has a security camera so you can do this at grocery stores or any of your favorite hangouts. Take advantage of those surveillance devices and give the guards a laugh or two. Look right into the security camera and use it as a mirror while you do some scratching, squeeze a zit or pick your nose.
Don't try this if your girlfriend is with you, unless you're tired of the relationship.

I'm not sure about the sanity of the people who came up with the next few suggestions. I wouldn't stoop this low to do them, but hey, you may care to try some of these.

You can pull this off at department stores or supermarkets, provided your grocery store has layaway. Go to the service desk and ask the clerk to put a bag of M&Ms on layaway.
Just a note of caution: They may lay you away for a long time.

On this next one, the cops may be summoned. You may still want to give it a shot. Dart around the store suspiciously while loudly humming the theme from "Mission Impossible." You may arouse some suspicion, so make sure the music is from the TV show, not the movie.

This is probably best done in a furniture store. Unfortunately, you might have a tough time getting the sign in this business. Move a *CAUTION – WET FLOOR* sign to a carpeted area.

There's almost no limit to where you can try this next stunt. Some stores even hire people to walk around the store and assist bewildered shoppers. When a clerk asks if they can help you, begin to cry and ask, "Why can't you people just leave me alone?"
Recently someone may have been trying to chase me down in the supermarket. He kept yelling, "Sir, sir." I ignored him – I was never knighted so he couldn't have been talking to me.

I doubt that you can try this next stunt anymore. Requisites are that you need to get a job in a supermarket that has a one-way window in the meat department. This is the window that looks like a mirror to the shopper but if you are in the meat department, you can spy on the shoppers. I spent my college days working at a supermarket in Cheektowaga, a suburb of Buffalo. Some of my crazier co-workers headed to this part of the store and while the consumers were checking out the chickens, they would cluck like those fowl. The best part was seeing the expression on the buyers' faces and not breaking up and spoiling the fun.

Because I spent eight years in this grocery store, today, I really don't care for grocery shopping – I have no choice, though – and I don't recommend work in this environment, but you have to make a living. I'm not sure if the mirror / window thing still exists. However, if the opportunity prevails, you can make grunting sounds like a pig – just don't disrespect the sow – as shoppers check out the hams and pork chops. Now that I really think about it, why would you install this mechanism in the meat department anyway? Does management figure that women are going to stash a fryer in their purse or a roast in their handbag? Maybe they did it so the help could have some fun and I could write about it.

Pick the finest clothing store for this effort. Hide in the clothing rack and when people browse through say, "Pick me, pick me."
There's got to be a better way to get a date for Saturday night.

All stores have that annoying *muzak* playing but also from time to time someone will make an announcement over the public address system. When they do, assume the fetal position and scream "No! No! It's those voices again."
You'll probably have to find a new place to shop.

Here's another fun thing to do. Let's say you use mass transit and someone approaches you, asking if the bus or subway came yet. Tell them, "Sure, about ten minutes ago."

What better place is there to have some fun than at a bank? You may want to avoid trying this at the one you patronize, unless you're ready to close out your account. Today we are bombarded with beeps, blips, bells, horns, whistles and music we don't want to hear. If you buy groceries, gas or just want to get money from the ATM, you will hear one beep after another for just about any transaction you make.

You can annoy the tellers – who doesn't like to do that? – with the following small gesture. Bring two dabs of cotton with you and sometime during your withdrawal or deposit from the ATM, put them in your ears. Just after your transaction is done and your card is ready to be removed, don't take it just yet. Go get a withdrawal form or deposit slip and start to fill it out, taking as much time as you can. The beeping will be continuous, but don't worry – it won't bother you. Eventually someone will come over to the ATM. When they start to talk to you, pretend you're hard of hearing. You can also dally when you deposit an envelope and accomplish the same effect. After you enter the amount, the ATM will be beeping again – but you won't hear it – just drop the envelope on the floor and take your time retrieving it. Once again, a teller will make an appearance. Ignore the person but begin a conversation on the topic of your choice and continue with your end of the diatribe. Responses from bank personnel are neither necessary nor relevant. Eventually, pick up the envelope, put it in the slot, complete the transaction and before leaving, indicate to the person, who may still be close by, that your hearing is going. *Older people will have more success with this trick.*

If you live in an apartment complex and have neighbors who have done you wrong or you just can't stand, you can get even. First buy some type of amplifier for your phone. Just before leaving your abode for your vacation, connect it to your answering machine or phone in some way so that when your phone rings, it will be as loud as the New York City subway. Just one word of caution: make sure that it doesn't shatter the glass in your home. Most likely, you will get calls while you are gone. However, to make sure your phone did ring a few times while you were on holiday, you may want to dial it at least once.

For an even better effect, bypass the answering machine, if you can, so that you can let the phone ring thirty times or more in a row. Hang up the phone after a sufficient number of rings – you don't want the cops to break down your door.

You may want the ability to deactivate the speakers remotely. The best time to try this is just before you move to a new place – there may be no other option, as you could be evicted because of the noise.

I wish I had thought of this sooner, but you may be able to try it. Suppose your parents speak in more than one language. Assuming you have a Polish heritage, they might speak in that language as well as in English at the dinner table. If you really haven't a clue to what they are referring when they converse in Polish, most likely they're talking about you. Without telling them, take classes in the Mother tongue so that you will be bilingual. No one should complain if you try to better yourself in this regard.

Once you are comfortable in that language and can understand and speak it, after they make some derogatory comment about you, enter into the conversation in Polish. They should be pleased to hear that you are no longer a bilingual illiterate.

There's just one word of warning: you may inadvertently cause a heart attack, so be careful.

I believe my answering machine must be part politician – it can't be trusted. I bought a new one that I hope is more reliable. I didn't do this but you can try it, if you happen to have two answering machines. First, put the exact message on each device and set each for four rings. Hook them both up for business. You may need to do some tweaking. With two answering machines working for you, you have a better chance of never missing a correspondence again through your phone.

There's another benefit – callers will be greeted in stereo. They should like that. Actually, it could turn out more like a reverb, but that's not a bad thing either.

138

When you have a great deal of free time, phone someone and when you get his answering machine, in a rather gruff voice leave this message: "We'll be over tomorrow morning with the backhoe to start digging."
You can even do this for people you don't know. This idea is courtesy of David Letterman.

If you're really bored, my answering machine fiasco of a previous chapter gave me this idea. Dial random numbers – you need not even use the phone book. If someone answers, you can hang up or repeat saying, "Hello." Ignore whatever the person who answers is saying. Do this a few times and then hang up. If you happen to get a machine, repeat the same exercise. Another variation of this for people with time on their hands is to sing an aria when you hear a real person talking. Don't sing too much of it and you may want to use a phone other than your own.

15. Coming soon

Another example of missing intelligence is television. During the course of the year, you will see proposals for upcoming programs. Besides the serious ideas, individuals come up with their own possibilities for shows. These are spoofs but they're worth a few laughs even though some of these are much better than what turns up on the screen. What follows are my ideas for TV programs, movies and Broadway plays. I caution you, they need some development. Most likely they will never make it big time, and that's probably a good thing.

Samson & Son – sitcom where the Biblical character and his favorite child try to make a living and get a few laughs from the recycling business

Remember Lo Mein – arson at a restaurant in Chinatown ignites a war in this soon-to-be released flick

Pun & Tellall – new variety show in which this comedic duo rely on language for laughs but spare no one

Hello Trolley – new musical based on *A Streetcar Named Desire*

Menendezino County – parents are being brutalized and murdered, forcing the authorities to spend overtime pay on investigation – coming soon to the WB

Trash – motion picture where a dozen lives intertwine during recycling on a weekend in a suburb of New York City
Though well done – some critics call it garbage – not as great as the Oscar winner with a similar title

141

Heir – new Broadway musical in which the cast plays strip poker to see who gets the fortune

Working on the Cheney Gang – soon to be released as a movie – Dick tells Condi, Rummy and Ashy that he has found a more efficient way of making license plates

Forrest Bump – sequel relates his struggles with his newly-discovered vision problem as he continually walks into walls

Steal of Fortune – corporate executives meet to determine how they can get more money from the poor and middle class to line their pockets

Victor's Secret – after downloading porn and getting caught, Victor almost loses his job

Lay it on the Line – former corporate executive Ken tries to do an Enron to escape conviction – soon to be on Fox

Perle Harbor Revisited – new action adventure movie in exploding *cinotex* in which Richard finds another country to bomb

Cliffhanger – sitcom in which Cliff Claven counsels inmates but they all seem to be dying; the warden can't figure out where the prisoners are getting the rope

Rummaging For Answers – new sitcom where George, Dick and Don try to figure out why the deficit is so high

Bantam of the Opera – long running musical where the hero finally comes home to roost

142

I Don't Want Rice at My Wedding – the Bush daughters have a joint wedding – under one condition

Never Cry Wolfowitz - after American forces are withdrawn from Iraq, Paul is dropped off in the country with twenty cases of Bud as he begins research to see if the place is really Sunni
*The original title was to be **An American Wolfowitz in Baghdad***

Samson & Daughter – with the recycling business going into the dumpster, the old man and his other child try their hand at selling luggage

The Price Is Wrong – new game show where contestants have to guess the cost of the Iraq war – there are no winners

Beat the Croc – new reality game show in which contestants have to survive a weekend in the Everglades

The Scooter is Busted – Dick does all he can but realizes he will have to get a replacement on this episode of *The Right Wing*

Swiffer Boat Veterans for Truth – after being denounced as frauds, the perpetrators are forced into community service doing cleanup work

Beaglemania – new Broadway musical that hasn't quite caught on and seems to be going to the dogs

Leopardy – a new reality game show, which is a spin-off of *Survivor* – you can figure out the rest

Thank God for *Seinfeld* – one of the greatest comedy programs of all time. Unfortunately, when the characters on the show went their separate ways, they weren't very successful. Here are a few programs that might fare better.

The Merchant of Bennes – Shakespearean play that just opened in London starring Elaine as Portia

Uncle Leo Conservatives – new program about a group of lobbyists who do their eyebrows with magic markers and keep talking about a son named Jeffrey

Creamer – Cosmo changes his name slightly and starts his own dairy; people wonder where the milk is coming from

Stewman – Newman leaves the post office, buys out the Soup Nazi and adds a few more items to the menu

Where's Popi? – coming to ABC in June – people in the restaurant can't locate him
Have they checked out any of the sofas?

Runaround Susan – Susan fakes her own death after having second thoughts about marrying George – can you blame her – and quietly slips away to Minnesota and begins dating a host of guys
Since she's not really dead, this just might work.

Thousand Dollar Babu – after returning from exile, Babu abandons the restaurant scene and starts training as a boxer
Coming from the Far East, he wasn't interested in a great deal of money.

Banyon in a Sling – after challenging Jerry to a ski race for a meal, Banyon ends up with body damage
If you don't get the humor here, you need to watch more foreign flicks.

Poop Nazi – after selling out to Newman, the Soup Nazi gets a job doing Hemoccult testing at a lab in the Bronx

The Four Georges – after each is fired, Costanza, Steinbrenner, Jefferson and W share an apartment in Manhattan trying to make it on Social Security and disability payments

Yoda, Yoda, Yoda – George's girlfriend deserts him and takes up with a wise Master of the Force

Rusty Goes into the Energy Business – the relative of Mr. Ed gets tired of his job in New York
If I have to explain this one, you need to watch more episodes of Seinfeld.

Bigger is Better – for the new catalogue, Elaine introduces a line of extra large hats for those with big heads

George Goes to Boot Camp – thinking he signed up to study marine biology, George winds up in the Marines and is not happy

Jerryatricks in Jersey – Jerry, Elaine, George and Kramer spend their Golden Years in a Ridgewood Retirement residence; they introduce themselves each day
This program is brought to you by Geritol and Depends.

16. Smart questions

In this chapter I have included the answer to a question posed in *for seeing eye dogs only*. I almost called this part, *The Wright Questions* – a reference to the comedian Steven Wright. These are questions that he might have come up with.

They say there is no such thing as a dumb question. I beg to differ as I have been at meetings and conferences at which I heard many questions that should never have been asked. They indicated that the questioner must have fallen asleep for part of the discussion or that this individual wanted to keep the discussion going so as to avoid a "pop quiz." Another possibility is that the person wanted to impress others with his intelligence. Unfortunately, in this situation, the phrase, "People wondered if he lacked intelligence but then he spoke and removed all doubt," was fulfilled.

The questions that follow might indicate that I should have added a three-letter word ending in a double 's' between the two words of the title. However, I chose not to add it. All that follows points out the connection between intelligence, the English language and humor.

If electricity comes from electrons, does morality come from morons?
It certainly doesn't come from the Neo-Conservatives.

If a canine doesn't like the water, could you call him a *land rover?*

If spoiled milk tastes funny, why didn't Susan laugh when Kramer involuntarily offered her a greeting of that substance?

147

Is there a new book coming out soon called, *Car Crash Test for Dummies*?

Have you ever been in a dither?
What did it feel like and was it conventional?

If the Canadian dollar becomes worth more than the U. S. dollar, will the washing machine I use in my condominium finally accept Canadian quarters?
This will be answered in the sequel. Yes, there's enough missing intelligence out so that I can keep writing these books.

If I am traveling by myself on vacation, can I eat at a *family restaurant?*

If a guy steps out of his Honda SUV, would he be out of his *Element?*

Does Neville Mariner conduct the Academy of St. Martin in the Fields if it's raining?

If a hot, humid summer day followed by a cool night is said to be good sleeping weather, would a winter evening when the mercury hits fifty below zero be great sleeping weather?

Will there ever be a movie, *7 Half Sisters For 7 Half Brothers?*

Could you refer to a half sister as a .5 sister? Since half brothers are quite common, are there such things as three quarter brothers and third sisters?
If my mom had one more son, I would have had a third brother.

If a turtle doesn't have a shell, is he homeless or naked?

If I asked the bookstore saleswoman to direct me to the self-help section," wouldn't that defeat the purpose?

How is it possible to have a civil war?
Do it with squirt guns and plastic knives.

If a deaf person swears, does his mother wash his hands with soap?
*I don't like your **Tone** of voice.*

Will there be a time when Heather Locklear and Andie MacDowell won't be worth it?
I don't write the commercials; I only comment on them.

If you ate both pasta and antipasto, would you still be hungry?

Shouldn't "hemorrhoids" be called "asteroids?"

Why is it called tourist season if we can't shoot at them?
That really depends on where you spend your vacation.

Can we trust any data from the Pew Center?
I would think that it would have a foul odor.

Shouldn't Benjamin Netanyahu change his name?
*The first name is fine but I'm not sure of any surname that ends in "**Yahoo**."*

If Michelle and Cass weren't the lead singers, would the group have been called the *Papas and the Mamas*?

Is Atheism a non-prophet organization?
They don't get any holidays either.

If the police arrest a mime, do they tell him he has the right to start speaking?

If one synchronized swimmer drowns, do the rest drown, too?
Not the intelligent ones.

Does Rumsfeld use Dove soap?
Probably not – his choice is Kashmir Bouquet.

Why did the Hundred Years War last 116 years?
They were probably using the metric system for counting.

Why do Panama hats come from Ecuador?
Would it be because there are no unions in the latter country?

While we're south of the border, is Taco Bell a Mexican phone company?
Tinker Bell is another, but it needs work.

Why does catgut, whatever that is, come from sheep and horses?
Felines like to hoard stuff.

How come the Russians celebrate the October Revolution in November?
Give them a break - they haven't yet recovered from Octoberfest.

Why is a camel's hair brush made of squirrel fur?
I think the camels were on strike – you've heard of Luckies!

Will President Bush bomb the Canary Islands in order to deal with the threat of bird flu?
Not if there are quail there.

150

Why was King George VI's first name, Albert?
He was hiding from a car salesman.

If a purple finch is crimson, is a blackbird blue?
He will be after his nest gets torn down for condos.

Why do Chinese gooseberries come from New Zealand?
They probably don't have any of their own.

Did wounded combatants in the Civil War get Reconstruction surgery?
Only if they were injured close to the end of the war.

Is the color of the black box in a commercial airplane orange to throw off the terrorists?
That should work – that idea was thought up by the Department of Homeland Security.

What happens when a girl named Sunshine gets hired at Fantastic Sams?
They can't call her Harry.

Is Wendy's the best place for "finger food?" Where did that term originate?
Maybe someone in the restaurant complained about the food to the cook and he gave them the finger.

Can I swim in a sanitary sewer?
Maybe, once.

Do marathon runners with bad footwear suffer the agony of defeat?

I'm an underwriter at a Buffalo radio station. In Australia, do they call it overwriting?

Do I need to be an officer in the Army, Navy or Air Force to use a doctor who specializes in general dentistry?
The leaders get their cars from General Motors.

What good will a square meal be to a starving person with a round plate?
The answer is square plates – they can be used for box lunches as well.

Are there any guarantees for medical work? If not, why not?
Maybe that's why we have practicing physicians.

Isn't MIS management a pleonasm?
Well, most of the time, from what I have seen.

Is Meow Mix a CD for cats?
If so, it probably wasn't put out by Snoop Dogg.

Does Ice-T drink coffee?

Is Boyz II Men a day care center?
You may want to drop off the kids at a different place.

Does Ice Cube have a tough time in the tropics?
He probably doesn't need to order ice with his drinks.

When God rebuilt the temple, why didn't he contract out to Halliburton?
Maybe he knew they were connected to Cheney!

If W calls the people of Kosovo, the "Kosovians," can we call his family the "Bush leaguers (maybe Bush whackers is better)?"
These people from Kosovo are probably related to the Kevokians or the East Timorians.

Are the Dominican Republicans an ally of the Bush White House?
Maybe they're just a religious right order.

Why don't rice cakes have frosting?
Even if they did, I still wouldn't eat them

As kids, did Branch Davidian members play in tree houses?
That may be the root of the problem, but I will leave it to your research.

Where do the spots on pinto beans go after cooking?
Maybe they wind up on the epidermis of those who eat them, and that's where freckles come from.

If my diet consists almost exclusively of natural food, will I die of natural causes?
I take no chances – I stay away from health food stores.

If an earthquake hits right in the middle of a house, resulting in half on each side of the fissure but the house still intact, is this what is referred to as a "home stretch?"
Maybe it will just be a "broken home."

What does "He has a date with Destiny" mean?
He certainly didn't meet her at the church social and won't be bringing her home to meet his parents.

Can I go into a combination bookstore / grocery mart and ask for OJ with pulp fiction?

Does canola oil come from cannolis?
Yes, but not from the male species.

Can I use my AM radio in the evening?
I've been looking but can't find any PM radios.

Does the country Chad have a problem with their voting machines?
It certainly can't compare to Florida or Ohio.

Should I fire my masseuse if she rubbed me the wrong way?
Only if she didn't take the Discover Card for payment.

Speaking of which, did Christopher Columbus finance his trip to America with the Discover Card?
Queen Elizabeth wouldn't give him a Visa.

If a man and a woman are wrapped in a barcode, could you say they are "an item?"
I'll have to check that one out.

If a Buddhist refused his dentist's Novocain during root canal work, is that because he wanted to transcend dental medication?
His provider didn't cover it.

If I speak my mind, will I be speechless?
It didn't help for some of the people I know who never close their mouth.

Should I move if it's true that 90% of all crimes occur around the home?
I doubt that becoming homeless will help in this regard.

Is it true that when crazy people go through the forest, they take the psycho path?
What if no one blazed a trail?

Do you get holy water by boiling the hell out of it?

If something blows a person's mind, does that mean that he won't understand much of this book?

154

Does a backward poet write inverse?

Do Eskimos get Polaroids from sitting on the ice too long?
Perhaps they were sitting around waiting to see what developed?

Are Santa's helpers subordinate Clauses?
That's why Mrs. Claus refused duty on Christmas eve – she was a feminist.

Is cheese that isn't yours, nacho cheese?
Whose is it, then?

Is spoiled milk what you get from a pampered cow?
How do you get them to wear that underwear anyhow?

If you cross a snowman with a vampire, do you get frostbite?
I'm sure it will be bloody cold.

Was Sanka served on the Titanic.
Probably along with Dunkin' Donuts.

Did the Pilgrims' pants always fall down because they wore their belt buckle on their hat?
The natives didn't have that problem.

Did W. E. B. Dubois have internet access?
They discriminated against him so he couldn't get a provider.

Why is there a light in the fridge and not in the freezer?
That's so the nasty parrot doesn't thaw out.

Can I get a mortgage at the West Bank?
Only if there's no collateral damage.

155

Do bakers trade bread recipes on a knead-to-know basis?
This seems to be a rising problem.

Why does your OB-GYN leave the room when you get undressed if they are going to look up there anyway?
Maybe it's his first time.

How is it one careless match can start a forest fire, but it takes a whole box to start a campfire?
You're probably not using enough gasoline.

If an invisible man marries an invisible woman, will the kids be nothing to look at as well?
They'll certainly save a lot on clothes.

Are those who jump off a bridge in Paris in Seine?
Not nearly as crazy as bungee jumpers or those who climb walls of ice.

Is a man's home his castle, in a manor of speaking?
For a farmer, we need to talk about a manure of speaking.

Can we practice safe eating by using condiments?
Not if you go to a fast food place.

Should condoms be used on every conceivable occasion?
Only in condominiums.

Is a midget fortuneteller who escapes from prison a small medium at large?
They'll have a hard time finding him.

Will those who get too big for their britches be exposed in the end?
Certainly and that's only the tip of the iceberg.

156

Is the biggest advantage of going back to school as a retiree that if you cut classes, no one calls your parents?
You just need to make sure they're not in the same class.

Why is it that once you've seen one shopping center, you've seen a mall?

Will enjoying a book while sunbathing make you well red?
Reading any book about war will make you blue.

When two egotists meet, is it an I for an I?

Do retirees not mind being called *Seniors* because with it comes a ten percent discount?

Is it true that a bicycle can't stand on its own because it is two tired?
What about a bike with trainer wheels?

When a clock is hungry, does it go back four seconds?
Later on, it will relieve itself with thirds.

Why is it in a democracy your vote counts but in feudalism your count votes?
It didn't appear that the votes of many people counted in the last two presidential elections.

Why is it time flies like an arrow while fruit flies like a banana?
Maybe it has something to do with that lady and the ridiculous hat.

Do people in the glee club at Capella University sing *a capella*?

Is it true that a retiree's bedtime is three hours after he falls asleep on the couch?
Will you feel stuck with your debt if you can't budge it?

Why did he break into song even though he couldn't find the key?
He wasn't concerned with his keyless entry.

If quizzes are quizzical, what are tests?
I always thought they were a detriment to learning. Maybe pop quizzes are Popsicle.

Is a boiled egg in the morning hard to beat?
Not if you get it before the water starts to boil.

Do illiterate people get the full effect of Alphabet Soup?
Only for a short spell.

In his writing, did Ian Fleming have to use Bond paper?
It's difficult to find today – I guess 007 is out of date.

If I had my appendix removed, can I still add it at the end of my book?
Maybe I should just use a foot note.

If a prison inmate had his prosthetic leg confiscated after he used it in a prison brawl, would he be hopping mad?

Why are politicians' mothers so strong?
Maybe it's from raising dumbbells.

If a person winds up with shrapnel in his body from the war, will there be any problems if he goes to a magnet school?
His teacher may ask him to stick around after class.

This question that follows was posed by a friend of mine at an Army football game many moons ago. You will appreciate my reference to that celestial body in a moment. His question, "Why do people who pass gas say, 'Excuse me' afterwards? Wouldn't it be more beneficial to give advance notice? How about, 'Warning, warning?'"

So that's what those words meant on "Lost in Space?"

Let's stay with this for a while, despite the discomfort. Those two words might be a bit confusing after 9/11 with all the various levels of alert, such as orange and red. We may need to be more specific, such as *chili warning*, *chalupa warning* or *burrito warning*. Maybe a generic approach is what we want, such as *environmental warning* or *move over Fido warning*.

Once again, my thanks go out to Joe Bernardi, who answered the question from my 2005 book, "What do you call male ballerinas?" He wrote:

I have an answer to one of your questions: For years I have called male ballet dancers ballerinos. It hasn't seemed to catch on yet. I guess I need to tell a few more people.

Printed in the United States
204328BV00001B/613-705/P